RIVER TIME

Mindful Reflections
from the Upper Hudson

STORIES, POEMS, & PHOTOGRAPHS BY
Susan Meyer

Printed in the United States of America
ISBN: 979-8-9989420-0-6
Library of Congress Control Number: 2025915318

Published by River Light Press
an imprint of Clear Mountain Press
P.O. Box 102
Schuylerville, New York 12871

ADVANCE PRAISE FOR *RIVER TIME*

"Susan Meyer has created a luminous offering—a gentle weaving of mindfulness, nature, and soulfulness. Her stories, poetry, and photographs invite us to slow down, listen deeply, and remember our belonging to the living world. With reverence and insight, she reminds us that the river is not just a place of beauty, but a teacher of presence, resilience, and grace. This is a delightful book to savor slowly, like a quiet paddle on still water."

Mark Coleman

Author of *A Field Guide to Nature Meditation*

"*River Time* is a gift—far more than a meditation on River's wisdom, it's an embodied immersion into the solace, equilibrium and learning that proximity to water, nature and the sacred patterns within them offer. Weaving personal reflections, essays and poems, this book generously springs from the wellspring of the author's long apprenticeship with the river and those kindred creatures who cohabit it with her. It's lucid, accessible, eloquent and a much-needed medicine for navigating this precipitous time. Gift yourself, and savor it, dipping in as you feel called. You won't be sorry!"

Nina Simons

Co-founder, Bioneers & author of *Nature, Culture & the Sacred: A Woman Listens for Leadership*

"*River Time* is a gift of beauty and peace. Take your time as you journey on New York's Hudson River with the author. A photographer, Susan offers compelling views of river life. These are supplemented with her essays and poetry on kayaking, water lilies, herons, mindfulness, and even dredging. This book is a lovely gift to give yourself or water loving friends. Whatever page you open to, you will find a refreshing, captivating experience—much like the river itself."

Starr Regan DiCiurcio
Author of *Dwelling in Wonder*

For Jack,
my companion on the river of life
who loves the river as I do

and for everyone who has loved a river.

RIVER TIME SUPPLEMENTAL RESOURCES

Available at SusanTaraMeyer.com

- ❖ Book Club Kit
- ❖ Guided Meditations
- ❖ Photo Gallery
- ❖ Immersive Hudson River Videos

CONTENTS

Preface xi

PART ONE: THE MORE THAN HUMAN WORLD

Water Lily Wisdom 3
Sunlit Leaves 10
The Story of Patrick Cottonwood 14
Memorial Day Weekend.................................. 17
The Patterns of Living Things 20
Heron Medicine... 22
River Bugs 26
The Wisdom of Dragonflies............................... 27
Goose Inspiration 30
Great Blue Heron... 32
Dragonflies in December 37
Egret on the Shore....................................... 39
A Single Swan 41

PART TWO: THE HUMAN WORLD

At the Epicenter 45
Dredging Meets Patrick Cottonwood 48
Don't-Know Mind 52
Dredging the Depths...................................... 57
River Ancestors 60
Lewis Pugh's Historic Hudson River Swim 67
Fast Boats 72
What Do You See?.. 77
Different Views 81
Waiting to Cross 86

PART THREE: RHYTHMS OF THE RIVER

A Year of Sunrise Photography............................ 91
From Project to Practice.. 93
Three Ways to See a Sunrise................................. 96
Sleep and You'll Miss It.. 100
Fascinated by Ice 102
Shared Joy 106
Summer Solstice Sunrise 108
End of the Project.. 112
Lost and Found 116
Predictably, Spring... 120
On the River in the Morning.............................. 124
In the Morning Fog 126
Floating Under the Moonless Sky 128
Moonlit Symphony 132
Beads of Dew... 134
In the Morning Mist 136
Autumn Releasing Ritual..................................... 139
The Exquisite Angle 142
This, Too, Shall Pass 146

PART FOUR: THE INNER RIVER

Mindful Paddling.. 153
River Refuge.. 156
Endless Possibilities 159
Maybe.. 162
Reflecting Stillness 166
Tears 170
Seated by the River.. 172
Opening to the Soundscape 174
Back to the Senses.. 178
Let It Go, Let It Flow.. 180
Hold the Rope 182
Zoom Out... 184
Where Does the River Begin and End?............. 188
River Bliss.. 193

Epilogue.. 197
Notes 203
Acknowledgments 207
About the Author... 209

PREFACE

Dwell as near as possible to the channel in which your life flows.
—Henry David Thoreau[1]

WELCOME TO THE RIVER. I've lived on the banks of the upper Hudson for the past seventeen years. In that time, the river has been my teacher and therapist, mirror and muse. It's also been a refuge from the noise of the everyday world.

Our family moved here in the fall of 2008, just as I began my career as a kindergarten teacher. At the time, my children were in elementary and high school. That spring, we bought a couple of kayaks, and I brought my camera on the river to photograph whatever caught my eye. There was so much to see.

When I left the classroom several years later, I got more serious about photography. What began as contemplative practice evolved into more of a calling. Within a few years, I also began formal training to become a meditation teacher, after more than thirty years as a practitioner.

The river has taught me to be present, and it helps me glimpse the deeper currents of my own life. It is my peaceful, receptive place. Being on the water is a different experience than being on land. Floating and gliding replace the usual orientation of firm ground beneath my feet. The river transports me into a different mindspace in which the usual voices grow quiet, and the conditions arise for inspiration, insight, and guidance to be received.

On the river, my mind becomes more spacious, and the walls I usually carry within me begin to dissolve. I experience a sense of *interbeing*, or interconnectedness, far greater than the small sense of *me*, *my*, and *mine*. There is more space for stillness, peace, presence, and connection.

One afternoon in 2012, I was out on the river in a quiet moment when a whisper of a voice told me to write. I can't say whether it rose up from within, drifted through the air, or belonged to the river itself, but it felt like a full-bodied *yes*. Writing poetry had been a lifelong hobby, but this was different. I trusted the voice and began writing a blog called *River Bliss*, a name that captured the state of heart and mind I experienced on the river—that I wished could be bottled and shared. If more people could get a taste of river bliss, I thought, surely the world would be a more peaceful place.

Writing was a means to express what I love about and learn from the river, how I practice mindfulness on the water, and how I see the world through a mindful lens. Weaving together photography, mindfulness, and writing became my sweet spot and my passion. Eventually, I launched my current blog, *Seeing and Being*, on Substack.

Twelve years after that first whisper, I found myself at a crossroads in my work. I felt stuck in a rut and returned to the river, as I often do, to listen. In a moment of stillness, the guidance came, clear and strong, like The Voice in the movie *Field of Dreams*. It said: *Write the book*.

Over the years, I've shared many river stories in my mindfulness meditation classes. Participants encouraged me to gather the teaching stories into a book. I had wanted to write a book for a long time, but life always seemed to demand something else more urgently. So, the book stayed on the back burner.

Then, shortly after that moment of clarity, my husband, Jack, had a stroke. It hit me with the same intensity as my mother's death: the undeniable truth that life is short, and everything can change in a heartbeat. The time to write the book had come.

I began brainstorming stories to include and quickly assembled a long list. Many had already been written, scattered across blog posts, newsletters, and journals. For the next few months, I gathered and reread them. Whenever I questioned whether this was the right path, the same message returned: *Write the book.*

So, in the quiet of winter, while the river was frozen, I began working in earnest. I trusted that voice and the sense of inner knowing, just as the Hudson had taught me to trust the flow of river and life and to meet them with an inner *yes*.

At its heart, this book is a meditation on mindfulness: kind, curious, moment-to-moment awareness. Mindfulness helps me attune to the natural world and uncover insights in everyday encounters that reflect and reveal something deeper. The river becomes a metaphor for the mind, emotions, time, and transformation. Themes of impermanence, interbeing, patience, presence, equanimity, and gratitude flow throughout.

One of the guiding inquiries behind these writings is: *If nature is a mirror or messenger, what is it showing me?* I have come to believe that we notice things when they have a message for us. How many times do we walk past something without seeing it? Then one day, it stops us in our tracks, as if it had been waiting in plain sight for just the right moment.

This book is a collection of mindful reflections, short stories, poems, and photos. They are arranged with a visit to the river in mind. If you were to stop by, I would be excited to take the kayaks out and introduce you to my non-human fascinations on the river: the wildlife and plant life. Then I would tell you about the people of the river and the impact they have had. Settling in and becoming more comfortable, conversation would deepen, to the more subtle rhythms of the river. And then, per-haps sitting around a fire overlooking the river, we would shift from outer landscape to inner landscape: what the river can teach us about ourselves and the world.

The sections of the book reflect this sequence:

❖ **The More Than Human World** introduces the ani-mals, trees, plants, and insects who share the river, each playing a role in the unfolding of life and reminding us to slow down, to observe, and to recog-nize our place in the wider web of interbeing.

❖ **The Human World** contains stories of river people current and past, and the Superfund PCBs dredging project that took place just beyond our dock. These stories explore the ways humans interact with the river and with each other.

❖ **Rhythms of the River** reflects on the elemental rhythms and cycles of day and night, seasons, and water. These stories are invitations to trust the con-stancy within the changing patterns. You will find sev-eral stories from my yearlong Hudson River sunrise photography project here.

❖ **The Inner River** considers how the river becomes a mirror, not just for sky and trees, but for the mind itself. These stories offer a river-inspired illustration of mindfulness practice: the currents of thought, the art of seeing deeply, and the clarity that arises when we are truly present.

This book is not meant to be rushed through. It's meant to be dipped into, like returning to the riverside for a quiet moment of reflection. You can read the stories in any order. Simply open to a page and begin.

May these stories offer not just glimpses into one river, but doorways into your own sense of presence, wherever your life flows.

Susan

PART ONE

The More Than Human World

WATER LILY WISDOM

If I were to choose a symbol for my life, it would be a water lily, without a doubt.

I'd always heard that my name, Susan, is Hebrew for "lily." But only recently did I learn that it may be more specifically linked to the *water* lily and the *white* lily, depending on how the ancient Hebrew word *shoshannah* is interpreted. The more nuanced connection, from lily to water lily, struck a resonant chord. It brought to mind the large patch of white water lilies across the river from our house, in a spot I lovingly call the "river garden."

Although I often wished my parents had chosen a more unique name, perhaps I was perfectly named after all because I am completely captivated by water lilies. Over the years, I have explored them from every angle. In summer, I can't resist paddling over to visit my "water lily friends" whenever I am on the river. If the water is shallow enough, a passerby might catch a glimpse of me contorted in "water lily photography yoga" poses, trying to achieve the most pleasing compositions.

Time disappears when I am with the water lilies. That's what happens when we are fully present—attuned to the moment, connected to what we love, or when love reveals itself through something or someone we are truly awake to.

I have learned to set a timer if I bring my camera on the river and have somewhere to be. Otherwise, I tend to linger with the water lilies. It doesn't matter that I already have thousands of photos of them; I keep returning. If I'm running late on a summer day, there's a good chance you will find me in the river garden among the lilies, where time escapes me.

Out of the Mud

I'm in awe of how an exquisite white flower rises from the muddy depths below. It reminds me that we, too, grow from the mud of our human lives.

There is a tendency to see challenges and suffering as obstacles. However, they are essential to our growth, just as mud is essential to the water lily. A life without suffering would be a life without growth. We grow conscious through contrast.

Zen master Thich Nhat Hanh wrote a book called *No Mud, No Lotus: The Art of Transforming Suffering*.[2] Although water lilies and lotuses are technically different, the teaching still applies. The mud of suffering *belongs*. It is the foundation from which we flower.

Sometimes we get stuck in the mud. Instead of surrendering to the process of awakening and reaching toward the light, we linger in the comfort of familiar narratives about ourselves, others, and the world. Those stories cloud our perception.

Looking back at times when I've felt stuck, it's amazing how much of that suffering was shaped by my own mind: how I used it, how I related to my thoughts. *I* was the one holding myself back. Even more astonishing is realizing that I always had the power to step out of those muddy narratives and into the present moment. To wake up, as if from a dream, and see more clearly.

It all begins with awareness.

Toward the Light

Awareness is the first step toward liberation. We cannot transform what we don't notice. When we notice, with kindness and compassion, the stories we tell ourselves start to loosen. Real transformation becomes possible.

Presence, a word I use interchangeably with *mindfulness*, is the practice of meeting life with kind, curious attention, moment by moment. As presence deepens, we may grow tired of the old narratives that are variations on the same theme: *This isn't how life (or other people, or my body) is supposed to be.* Those judgments feed a sense of separation, superiority, or inadequacy. They do not serve our growth and freedom.

When we catch them arising, we can peek behind the curtain: *Hello, Ego. I see you. I see what you're doing. Thanks for trying to help. I've got this.*

The more we practice presence, the more momentum we build in choosing it over the trance of story. Awakening begins to feel more natural. Sometimes I catch myself on the verge of spinning a story about a person, a situation, or myself, and an inner alarm goes off: *Story!* That moment of recognition is enough to return me to the immediacy of birdsong, flowing river, drifting clouds, wind in the trees.

Being caught in a story is like a water lily bud submerged beneath the surface, stuck in the current of thought. But when we become aware of the water around us—our mental environment—we can stop identifying so strongly with it and begin to see the filter that distorts our view. As awareness grows, we keep reaching toward the light, where deeper insight and wisdom await, and blooming happens naturally.

The truth is, our minds don't need to work so hard. There is a more easeful, balanced way to navigate life that opens new channels of perception. We don't have to stay trapped in the murkiness of our stories.

With practice, we develop the capacity to notice what is happening in our minds. Like a water lily rising through the water, we can choose to keep stretching upward. We can shift our relationship with thought and use it for growth instead of limitation. We can relax the grip of overthinking and free ourselves from disempowering beliefs or unhealthy situations.

Like the water lilies, we are invited to rise from the mud, grow through the water, and bloom in the open air, where we can touch the warmth of the sun without the veil of stories that distract us from life itself. We are invited to bloom. To become more than a closed bud. To flower. To be part of the pollinating world and inspire others to do the same.

Our blooming is evidence that transformation is not only possible; it is our nature. The blueprint lives within us.

We Are Not Alone

Above the surface, each bloom appears separate, floating individually. But beneath the water, the water lilies are connected by stems and rooted in deep rhizomes.

As I paddle carefully through the lily pads, I notice how everything is intertwined. Disturb one, and everything around it moves. I search for the best angle for a water lily portrait, but even the slightest shift of my paddle changes everything: the light, the shape, the way the lily rests on the water.

The lily pads gather sunlight and nourish the flowers, helping them grow and bloom. The first time I looked closely at the intricate veins of a lily pad, I was amazed by how closely they mirrored the design of the flower. They are *that* interconnected.

A glimpse beneath the surface offers the insight that, like the water lilies, we are not alone. We are part of the same ecosystem, deeply connected to all of life. We have help. We are in this together. Our struggles are shared.

Our suffering is the mud we rise from, individually and collectively. It serves a purpose. It is not a flaw but the ground we share: the fertile soil of our becoming.

The Importance of Rest

The first time I visited the water lilies last summer was just after the solstice. I'd stayed up too late and missed the sunrise. By the time I got on the river, the afternoon heat had already settled in, and most of the lilies had begun to close for the day. Their timing reminded me of the importance of rest.

Water lilies awaken shortly after sunrise. Each morning, the flowers rise to meet the light and unfurl from tight green buds. By mid-afternoon, they begin to close and retreat beneath the surface. The next day, they rise again. This rhythm continues for about four days, until they return to the mud and decompose.

The lilies' daily cycle of opening and closing, retreating and rising, offers a lesson in balance. Their blooming depends on rest and restoration. They rise when the light is right, and when the time comes, they sink back into the cool, shaded water. In the pressured pace of modern human life, I aspire to live like that: to honor the natural ebb and flow of my energy and sense when it is time to rise and when it is time to rest.

Bloom Where You Are Planted

When I first became enamored with the white water lilies on the river, I was struck by the contrast between their delicate beauty and the polluted riverbed in which they were rooted: a riverbed contaminated with PCBs.

In a world full of uncertainty and toxicity, it's easy to forget that beauty can still emerge from difficult circumstances. Yet here we are, like the lilies, growing in challenging conditions.

We don't have to give in to despair. We can choose to find strength, hope, and creativity within ourselves. When we do, we open more fully to life and to expressing the goodness that lives in us. We begin to share our own fragrance of kindness, beauty, and inspiration with the world.

And in doing so, we uplift others. We show the next generation that blooming is possible. We help guide them upward, toward the light of their own potential.

The real challenge lies in the daily choice to bloom: to express our true, boundless nature instead of withering in the bud of fear. It's about claiming our power, one moment at a time, and allowing life to move through us.

Just like the Hudson River water lilies, we can bloom beautifully, even in polluted waters. We can choose to bloom where we are planted.

SUNLIT LEAVES

One morning, just like that,
I saw the river flowing
in sunlit leaves, as if the leaves
became the river, tinted green.
The effect was so remarkable
that I wondered how I hadn't
noticed it before in my
fifty-something years of living.

That morning, I didn't bring
a proper camera with me
and returned the next day
better prepared to record
the dance of light and shadow
projected onto the oak leaves
above the river—
but it was not the same.

The wind was too gusty,
and the river flowed too fast.
The leaves blew and curled
in the summer breeze,
and the angle of sunlight
wasn't quite right.

I returned again and again.
Sometimes the river flowed gently
as it had that first day,
but there was not enough sunlight.

Then I understood
why I hadn't noticed before:
We must be in the right place
at the right time,
with exactly the right conditions—
and receptive—
for something new to reveal itself
and capture our attention.

And because of this knowledge,
and because I've learned to bring
the lens of loving awareness
to my life and all its blunders,
I don't regret
not discovering sooner
the river in a sunlit leaf
or the truths of a personality.

Epiphanies happen
when we are still enough,
at just the right angle
in relation to light and form—
when conditions are right
and our senses are open.

Our willingness
is only part of the equation;
timing and alignment matter, too—
and being ready
and prepared.

Fascinating things
and revelations
hide in plain sight
until the time is right.

And then we can't unsee them.

What we are drawn to
in the world around us
reflects what is arising
within us.

THE STORY OF PATRICK COTTONWOOD

There are many eastern cottonwood trees lining the river, and I have spent countless hours observing and appreciating them. Their energy is powerful, and their life cycle is intriguing. I learned that cottonwood trees are sacred to the Lakota people and central to their Sundance ceremonies. Given their presence and vitality, their spiritual significance wasn't surprising.

One year, spring arrived early, and I started kayaking in March—something rare. As I paddled along the shore, I photographed various trees to share their life cycles with my kindergarten students on our classroom SMART Board. I captured images of maple, oak, and willow trees, as well as a mystery tree that took some time to identify. Beneath the canopy of this tree, I'd float in my kayak, reflect, and find answers to unspoken questions.

That mystery tree turned out to be an eastern cottonwood.

In one of the photos, my students noticed patterns of five buds grouped together, resembling a starfish. Inspired by a character from *SpongeBob SquarePants*, they dubbed it "the Patrick tree." Each day, they eagerly asked if I had more pictures of Patrick. Naming the tree was a turning point that brought the tree to life for them. Even I began to think of Patrick as having a personality and felt drawn to learn more about him.

Although still unsure of what kind of tree Patrick was, I continued documenting his changes. I photographed the drooping strands of tiny flowers called *catkins* and the emergence of tiny, unfurling leaves. By this point, my curiosity had deepened, and after some research, I finally identified Patrick as a cottonwood. The next day, I excitedly shared my discovery with the children, telling them I had learned Patrick's last name. From then on, he was known as "Patrick Cottonwood."

As Patrick's leaves grew larger, deepened in color, and lost their waxy sheen, I delved further into the cottonwood's cultural significance. I learned that one reason the tree is considered sacred is that its leaves are thought to have inspired the design of the Lakota tipi. According to *The Cottonwood Tree: An American Champion* by Kathleen Cain, the Lakota holy man, Black Elk, explained that children would fashion tiny playhouses from cottonwood leaves, which eventually led elders to construct full-sized tipis.[3] I also read that when an upper branch of a cottonwood tree is cut, the cross-section reveals a five-pointed star, which perhaps explained the star-like pattern of Patrick's buds.

I discovered that cottonwood trees are either male or female and that the name *cottonwood* comes from the fluffy seed clusters produced by female trees in the fruit stage. I was eager to see which cottonwood trees would go through this stage as the season progressed. When Patrick didn't produce the cottony seeds, I confirmed that he was, indeed, male. Across the river, I spotted a female cottonwood covered in green fruits containing those delicate seed clusters. The children named her "Fluffy."

I explained to my students that Fluffy was Patrick's girlfriend and that he sent gifts of pollen to her through the wind. In return, she released cottony seed fairies into the air when her fruits opened. The children were enchanted by this story, and their enthusiasm reinforced something I deeply believe: When a teacher is genuinely passionate about a subject, it sparks children's curiosity and engagement.

On windy days in late spring, I love paddling near the cottonwoods, watching the seed fairies drift in the wind and float in the current. Cottonwoods, like aspens, have leaves that quiver and rustle in the breeze. When I approach Patrick Cottonwood in my kayak, his heart-shaped leaves appear to wave a welcoming hello.

Throughout the summer, Patrick remains largely unchanged. But by autumn, his leaves begin turning gold, much like human hair grays with age and wisdom. Slowly, they release one by one until a late October breeze leaves him bare, ready for his winter rest. When spring arrives, the cycle begins again. I watch millions of cottonwood seeds float on the river in late spring and wonder where the next generation of cottonwoods will take root.

I also wonder where my kindergartners' lives will lead them. The "Patrick" class has now graduated from high school, and I'm happy to still be in touch with some of them and their families.

Years later, Patrick Cottonwood remains my favorite tree on the river. His low branches that once gave me an up-close view of his buds, catkins, and leaves were removed in preparation for the PCBs dredging. But that's another story. Even now, every time I paddle by, I wave and call out, "Hello, Patrick Cottonwood!" I think of that kindergarten class and feel a smile warming my heart.

MEMORIAL DAY WEEKEND

I've regularly paddled the same four-mile stretch of the river for more than seventeen years. In my kayak, I notice a lot that is happening around me. Yet somehow, there is always something new that's hard to believe I hadn't noticed before. When something really jumps out at me, I wonder: What kind of message does it bring? If nature is a teacher or mirror, what is it showing me?

My mother passed away in the early morning hours after Memorial Day 2014. On Memorial Day weekend six years later, I was paddling my usual route, soaking in the beauty of the season. At some point, John Denver's song "Sunshine on My Shoulders" started playing in my head. It was one of her favorites. I even sang it out loud for the birds and trees. My mom had been a huge John Denver fan, and the song made me think of her. It felt like she was with me.

As the song looped in my mind, something along the riverside pulled my attention so strongly that I stopped paddling. A cluster of tiny flowers was growing straight out of a rocky wall. Life was blooming all around me, but these delicate, blue blossoms stood out as if they were calling to me.

I hadn't noticed them before. It was as if the rock itself were offering me a bouquet. I lingered there for a while, taking in every detail of these unidentified flowers.

When I started paddling again, I headed toward a small waterfall in the distance, well beyond my usual turnaround point. A single white feather appeared on the water, and I stopped to observe it. It floated around my kayak almost playfully, moving as if to get my attention. Then it drifted down the river in the opposite direction I was headed. Curious, I turned around and followed it, watching as it glided around fallen trees and eventually came to rest, as though it had accomplished its mission: to lead me back home.

It was a sunny, blue-sky day. I hadn't realized my skin was already beginning to burn—and I hadn't packed sunscreen. If I had gone all the way to the waterfall, I would have gotten scorched. The feather changed my course.

When I got home, my son told me he'd had a vivid experience in which my mom placed her hands on his shoulders and sent a radiant warmth through his body. I knew that feeling. I'd experienced the same thing after she died, in a dreamlike state I can still remember. My sister had, as well. It was the most delightful feeling.

Touched, I called my daughter, to share her brother's experience. However, before I could bring it up, she mentioned feeling a beautiful light and warmth come over her that same day, along with a strong sense of my mother's presence.

The tiny, blue flowers were so alluring that I returned the next day with my camera. I still didn't know what kind of flowers had caught my attention. But when I posted the photo online, someone commented with their name: forget-me-nots.

Moments like these are hard to explain but deeply felt. They remind me that there is more going on than meets the eye, that relationships don't end with physical death, and that nature is always speaking, if we are quiet enough to hear. Whether through a song, a flower, a feather, or a feeling, something tender and sacred made itself known to me that day, in a way I couldn't miss.

The Patterns of Living Things

After ten years of photographing
water lilies, one day I saw it:
The patterns on lily pads
mirror the water lilies themselves.
How had I not noticed before?

The patterns imprinted on living things—
cottonwood and maple leaves
carrying the blueprint of their trees,
subtle designs of connection and belonging—
are everywhere.

Our breath echoes
the rhythm of ocean waves.
And like white water lilies
resting in full bloom on the water,
we, too, rise from the mud toward
the light and bloom.
They show us the way
and reflect our journey.

Great blue heron,
still as a statue at river's edge
reminds me over and over
of the power of stillness.

Wherever we come face-to-face
with ourselves in nature,
we are home—part of
a vast belonging.
And isn't that
what we truly long for?

HERON MEDICINE

Along with water lilies, great blue herons have been my most abiding interest on the river. I've spent many hours observing them, with and without my camera. They've taught me about steady presence, patience, trusting inner knowing, and the wisdom of moving on.

Herons don't linger where conditions no longer serve. Migratory by nature, they offer one of their clearest teachings: knowing when it is time to go.

Sometimes I've paddled alongside one walking the shoreline, but more often it feels like a game of hide-and-seek. The heron hides, on the ground or in a tree, and I seek. We might play this game for the entire length of my paddle. I swear that bird can become invisible at will.

Even when I track where it lands and try to keep the spot in sight, I'm often surprised by the sudden squawk and whoosh of wings when I get closer than I realized. Then, with slow, powerful strokes, the heron lifts off in search of a quieter place. In flight, herons look so focused, as if guided by a deep inner compass.

They have a strong sense of boundaries and are acutely sensitive to movement. Yet when I'm absorbed in photographing water lilies and a heron flies past with a squawk, it almost seems like an invitation into another round of hide-and-seek. Surely that's not the case, but sometimes I can't resist. *Game on.*

Often, I don't even know a heron is near until I hear its cry. If it's visible, I'll stop paddling, hoping to stay unnoticed long enough to watch. But herons on the river don't often tolerate close company. Eventually, they take off, putting more distance between us. It's easy to underestimate how attuned animals are to our presence.

The great blue heron is a majestic figure, standing motionless for long stretches like a statue charged with awareness. A solitary hunter, the heron embodies independence, focus, and self-trust. When I feel restless or pulled by others' opinions, I conjure its image. It reminds me to return to presence and follow my inner wisdom.

Herons usually keep their distance, but sometimes they let me come closer—always on their terms. Once, I paddled toward the water lilies and was startled to find a heron just yards away. I don't know why I was allowed so near, but it was an opportunity to capture a few close-up photos and absorb its presence. A powerful zoom lens helps me respect their space, but being close enough to feel the heron's essence without crossing an invisible boundary is something else entirely. Clearly, they want to hunt in peace. Yet being near them feels like receiving medicine: a transmission of their patient, steady presence.

I have watched herons so closely that I recognize the subtle shifts that precede flight. They orient toward the source of the sound or movement—head turning slightly, body alert—gauging whether it signals danger. Then comes a gathering of energy before they lift off with deliberate power.

Unlike geese, who travel in groups, herons are usually spotted alone on the river. As an introvert, I find kinship in their solitude. They remind me of the value of space and the strength of trusting one's instincts: an antidote to groupthink.

Though calm in stillness, they strike with breathtaking speed when the moment is right. I've watched in awe as their sharp beaks dart into the water and emerge with fish that disappear down the curved tunnels of their neck.

Spotting a heron is often the highlight of my river time. Observing one is a meditation. Their presence draws me into my own.

I have spent countless hours learning from great blue herons. I admire their steady concentration and their readiness to move on when a place no longer suits—whether to a quieter stretch of shoreline or migrating to warmer climates when the season shifts.

There are life lessons herons have taught me that I am still learning to embody. In my own life, I've often overstayed in situations that didn't serve me. It felt safer to stay than to face the discomfort of change or risk disappointing others. But herons do not apologize for needing space. They do not wait for permission. They simply know when it is time to go.

If something isn't working, try something else. It's a lesson that stands in contrast to what the water lilies have taught me about blooming where you are planted. Both are true, just at different times. The key is sensing what the moment calls for. Is this a water lily moment calling for rooted resilience? Or a heron moment, asking me to move toward what's next?

RIVER BUGS

One summer morning while kayaking, I noticed a particular type of bug must have just hatched. Every few minutes, I was swarmed by them. Some landed on my legs, others on my arms, and a few even found their way onto the floor of my kayak. I swatted and shooed, but more kept coming.

At some point, I realized I was focusing more on the bugs than on the considerable beauty around me. My mind had been distracted, and in the process, I wasn't fully present in paddling or moving forward.

I also noticed something else: Because of the bugs, I didn't stop to float, as I usually would. Floating is one of the most peaceful, blissful experiences. But that morning, I kept paddling. If I stopped, the bugs would swarm me. As a result, I covered more distance in less time than usual. My arm muscles were constantly engaged, giving me a better workout than I would have gotten if I had paused now and then to relax and bask.

Perhaps we can find value in the "bugs" that show up in our lives. They make us stronger and prevent us from becoming too comfortable. They keep us moving forward, helping us arrive sooner at our destination. When we meet them with acceptance, we can appreciate the journey more fully, remaining mindful of the goodness around us rather than consumed by resistance.

THE WISDOM OF DRAGONFLIES

There is a rocky sliver of a beach a short distance upriver that is just large enough to pull my kayak onto and do some walking meditation back and forth for fifteen to twenty paces. It's one of my favorite spots when the water is low enough to access it.

One day, while practicing walking meditation, my attention was drawn to dragonfly exuviae (exoskeletons) attached to the rocky wall I walked alongside. They were well camouflaged, hidden in plain sight. They are often visible on lily pads and stems of river plants, but I was able to examine the ones on the rocky wall more closely and became engrossed.

I noticed the opening from which the dragonflies had emerged and imagined them resting on their exuviae, adjusting to their new bodies—and wings! Once bound to the water, they had transformed into something entirely new.

Photography has always been a spiritual practice for me. The images I am drawn to reveal insights into the questions I carry. They are like mirrors offering glimpses into myself and the world around me.

The dragonfly exuviae seemed to carry a message, though I couldn't put my finger on it. And anyway, walking meditation isn't about analyzing; it's about presence. I set aside the thought and simply smiled whenever a dragonfly zipped by.

Later, as I reviewed the day's images, the metaphor emerged. The exuviae spoke of transformation, of molting and growth, of shedding the familiar and stepping into something new. I had just released myself from a couple of part-time jobs and stepped fully into the work I felt deeply called to do. Like the dragonfly,

I was moving into the next phase of my life's journey. Dragon-flies molt many times throughout their lives, each time a new beginning. Their abandoned exuviae reflected my own transition.

The next day, something happened that stirred feelings of grief, which I met with mindfulness. *Hello, Grief. What can I learn from you today? What do you want me to know?*

I placed my hands tenderly over my heart, where the sorrow had settled. As I sat with it, an image arose in my mind, gaining clarity like an old Polaroid instant print developing. It was the shape and color of a heart. Then, just like the dragonfly exuviae, the heart broke open, and from it, a winged being emerged. A dragonfly, light and unfettered, lifted into the air—a shimmering teacher of transformation.

A voice from within me spoke: *You are so much more than this challenge, which you will rise to. More than these feelings, which will pass.*

As I watched the dragonfly dart around in my mind's eye, an answer formed. My heartspace felt lighter. I had a way forward.

And then I understood more about the exuviae symbolism: When the world breaks my heart, maybe something new, wiser, and more expansive is hatching from the rupture. If I take the time to lean in and listen, it will show me the way.

GOOSE INSPIRATION

Stand through life as firm as a rock in the sea, undisturbed and unmoved by its ever-rising waves.

—Hazrat Inayat Khan[4]

I often think back to a Canada goose I observed many years ago on the river. At the time, I was generally more reactive to boats speeding by, leaving strong wakes that crashed toward the shore. Some days, I was more accepting, paddling through the turbulence with a sense of calm or confidence. Other days, irritation arose when boaters passed too quickly, showing little regard for the kayakers on the water.

How we perceive situations and others is influenced by what we carry with us on this river of life. Over time, I realized that I couldn't control the speed of the boats, but I could control my response to them and the skill with which I navigated the rough waters.

One afternoon, as I was heading back to the dock, a motorboat sped by, sending strong waves rippling through the water. Although I had been in a peaceful state of mind, a wave of irritation began to rise within me.

As the wake surged forward, I spotted a lone adult goose gliding on the water. Despite the approaching turbulence, the goose remained perfectly calm and unruffled. She floated effortlessly over the waves, apparently not bothered in the least. She didn't fly away, spread her wings, or make a sound. Instead, she moved with grace, riding each wave, completely at peace.

I continued to watch the goose even after the waters had settled. She circled near the dock where I was sitting, then slowly made her way upstream. I watched her for as long as I could, absorbing her calm energy, letting the image imprint on my mind. It was something I could recall whenever I faced life's turbulent waters.

And I have. That was many years ago, but when I find myself reacting strongly to circumstances beyond my control, I think of that goose and remind myself to embody her grace and centered stillness.

GREAT BLUE HERON

As autumn temperatures
begin to dip, I wonder:
When will be the last time
I see his distinct form
accenting the river landscape—
for good, I mean.

Sometimes I suspect he's gone,
but then I'll glimpse him
lingering in a quiet corner.
He hasn't yet migrated
away from the river,
but I anticipate his longer,
inevitable absence.

Each sighting becomes
more precious
as his departure looms.
Drawn to his form—
the S-curve of his neck,
his deeply focused posture—
I will seek him as long as
there is something left
to learn from him.

He does not meet my gaze
with the interest I rest
on him, for he is wild,
focused on survival.
I follow him up
and down the river
in a game of hide-and-seek
that makes river time
more exciting.

But when I set my sights
on glimpsing him,
what else am I not seeing?
When I spend my time
chasing him,
what else am I not doing?
Many evenings, I return home
wondering what joys I missed
while pursuing a creature
so aloof.

I follow him to places
I otherwise would not have seen,
though he gives no sign
he wants to be followed
or even adored.
Perhaps he finds
the attention annoying.

But would it matter?
For he is a master of leaving,
and he will go—
when the conditions
no longer suit him.
His nature is to migrate
rather than adapt.

Steely eyes, rigid posture—
solitary hunter is focused.
He does not notice me
until I have crossed
his invisible boundary.
Then he lifts his head,
and I know what comes next:

Those heavy wings will
unfold and beat the air—
swift, unapologetic.
He will rise, eyes fixed ahead
on the next best place
to touch down and hunt.

Every year at this time,
the heron departs, for he
cannot find sustenance here
when the season changes.
And each time
I must let him go,
turn my mind to more
constructive matters.

Yet giving him my attention
was worthwhile—for he
has taught me much:
how to leave a place
I once felt at home
when my soul has moved on
and beckons me to follow,
how to trust I will find
something new and hopeful.

Great blue heron
has taught me to let go.

DRAGONFLIES IN DECEMBER

One winter when I was teaching kindergarten, tragedy struck the family of one of my students. In searching for stories to support grieving children, I came across a gem of a booklet by Doris Stickney called *Water Bugs and Dragonflies*.[5]

The story imagines a colony of water bugs puzzled by the disappearance of their friends who climb a lily stalk and never return. They agree that the next one to go up will come back and tell the others what happens. But when it happens again, the bug transforms into a dragonfly, able to zip through the air and see from above, but no longer able to return beneath the surface. Even if his friends could see him looking down at them, they wouldn't recognize him in his new form. He realizes they will each have to make their own journey to understand what lies beyond.

I was deeply moved by this metaphor from the natural world. The dragonfly life cycle offers a beautiful way to explain death to children.

After reading the booklet, I recalled a recent afternoon when I paddled to the lily pads and arrived just in time to witness a newborn dragonfly fall from its exoskeleton—which still clung to a reed—onto a lily pad. It was pale and colorless, looking completely disoriented. It lay motionless, and I wondered if it would be okay, hoping the fall hadn't harmed it. The booklet mentioned this moment, suggesting it is a normal part of the transition.

It was an honor to witness this seemingly small yet profound event in the natural world.

Then I noticed something that had been overlooked before: numerous dragonfly exuviae clinging to reeds and water lily stalks all around me. They were completely still, and I had mistaken them for living creatures. But they were only empty shells, ghosts of former selves. I became fixated on photographing them.

Later, as I reflected on *Water Bugs and Dragonflies* with the grieving child in mind, I realized the exuviae held an even deeper meaning. They could help explain to a child that the body of a deceased loved one is merely a shell, not to be confused with the living presence they had known and loved. The essence of that person, like the dragonfly, has moved beyond what we can see.

EGRET ON THE SHORE

During the summer of 2023, ocean advocate and endurance swimmer extraordinaire, Lewis Pugh, swam the entire length of the Hudson from the Adirondacks to New York City. The morning he was scheduled to pass by our house, my eyes were constantly on the water, until I finally was able to get in my kayak. With my camera equipped with a 400mm lens in a waterproof sack, I paddled upriver until the spot where he would begin his daily swim was in sight. But there was no sign of him. I wondered if I had somehow missed him or if he was running behind schedule.

While waiting, I became transfixed by a great white egret on the shore. I floated silently near the egret for several minutes, my zoom lens allowing me to keep a respectful distance. It had been years since I had photographed an egret on the river. I composed shot after shot, watching the elegant curve of his neck shift into different shapes. But my favorite image of the day was one in which his neck wasn't visible at all.

At first, I couldn't put my finger on what it was about the image that gripped me. But then, in an instant, I understood. There I was, admiring this stunning bird as he seemingly gazed at his reflection in the water. Of course, the egret was scanning for fish, not focused on his reflection—but the visual metaphor struck me. The surface of the water was rippled, distorting the reflection beyond recognition. The egret couldn't see the beauty I saw in him. From his perspective, he would have seen something entirely different and skewed.

I felt a pang of recognition. How often do we fail to see clearly our own beauty and magnificence? How often do we watch someone we care about struggle to recognize their own worth, when it is so clear to us? The image felt like the river holding up a mirror, showing me my own patterns.

If only the water were still and clear so the egret could see himself as I saw him. Then again, maybe self-consciousness is just a human affliction.

A Single Swan

In the fall of 2020, a trumpeter swan arrived on the river. A towering, white figure, it stood out among the gaggle of Canada geese with whom it kept company.

This was the first and only time I've seen a swan on the river. It stayed for a few days, and during that time I made several attempts to photograph it. Unfortunately, I didn't have a powerful enough zoom lens to capture wildlife from a distance. I did my best with the lenses I owned, but the swan wouldn't let me get close enough for a decent shot.

On a foggy and frosty Halloween morning, after trying to photograph the swan from my kayak, it flew away and didn't return. I felt disappointed, having squandered an opportunity that landed almost literally right on my doorstep.

Over the winter, I reflected on the missed chance and weighed the benefits and costs of buying an expensive zoom lens. I got clear on what mattered to me: What do I really want to photograph? What brings me joy?

I considered the limitations of my current gear and situations in which a more powerful zoom lens would be beneficial. For example, I could fill the frame with the moon or distant mountains and photograph water lilies from different perspectives even when the water was too low to get close. I imagined the satisfaction of being ready to photograph wildlife whenever I encountered it on the river. The missed opportunity still stung, but it offered clarity about what is important to me as a photographer.

On the first day of spring, I finally bought the lens. A few days later, Jack and I were walking along the canal, and I spotted a white swan on the far side. This time, I had the lens with me! Feeling triumphant, and a little puzzled by the swan's odd movements, I composed a few pictures, then continued our walk.

When I got home and zoomed in, I had a good laugh: I'd photographed a plastic decoy swan. But the image was crisp, and I was equipped for wildlife photography!

Though I hadn't been able to photograph the real swan to my satisfaction, that experience was the catalyst for me to get clear on what mattered and finally invest in the wildlife lens. Over the years, it has brought me so much joy. I've been able to photograph countless subjects well, while maintaining a respectful distance. The price tag? Worth every penny.

That swan was a mindfulness bell, pointing me to what truly matters. The contrast between the picture I could have taken with a better lens and the photos I actually took spurred me to act. Even though I missed out on photographing the swan on the river to my satisfaction—and I've yet to see another swan there—the missed opportunity was still valuable for the clarity it provided.

PART TWO

The Human World

AT THE EPICENTER

For about three decades, until 1977, the General Electric Company (GE) discharged an estimated 1.3 million pounds of polychlorinated biphenyls (PCBs) into the Hudson River, just miles upstream from where we now live. At the time, this kind of industrial waste disposal was common practice, before the federal ban on PCBs in 1979.

In 1984, the Environmental Protection Agency (EPA) designated a 200-mile stretch of the Hudson River as a Superfund Site. It was one of the largest hazardous waste sites in the country due to PCB contamination. Between 2009 and 2015, a forty-mile section underwent massive environmental dredging to remove contaminated sediment. Conducted by GE under EPA oversight, the cleanup extracted about 2.7 million cubic yards of PCB-laden material.[6]

Dredging took place twenty-four hours a day, six days a week, for about eight months a year. In 2013, it arrived at our doorstep. We had been loosely tracking its progress and assumed we had another year before the mechanical dredges reached our section of the river. But we were wrong. And we braced ourselves.

One spring day, just twenty minutes into a routine paddle, I rounded a bend and came face-to-face with dredging machinery, closer than I'd realized. Within a month, a parade of barges and workboats passed by our house day and night. Eventually, water quality monitors dotted the river in front of our house, their tips blinking like fireflies.

I learned these were *near-field monitors*, collecting daily data for lab analysis. Both air and water quality standards were strict. If PCB levels exceeded limits, operations would be altered.

Airborne PCBs and *resuspension* of PCBs in the water (stirring up of sediment) were my greatest fears as the project got closer to us. Learning about the safety measures in place helped ease my concerns, though I remained wary. Even before the dredging, I had erred on the side of caution, avoiding direct contact with the water. If any part of me touched the water, I would take a shower.

In every conversation with the EPA representative, I was reminded of how sophisticated the technology is. The EPA's public data portal detailed how the dredging was measured and monitored. Though the process looked sloppy, the excavator's clamshell bucket was designed to seal in the contaminated sediment before bringing it to the surface. Seeing the workers on the barges and boats wearing only hard hats and neon vests—no air masks or hazmat suits—was strangely reassuring.

For the rest of the season, Sunday was our only paddling day of the week because it was when the dredging jaws rested. One Sunday morning in early August, when the water was calm and boat traffic was light, Jack and I ventured out in our kayaks. Rounding the bend, we found ourselves staring at a fleet of several enormous dredging barges. It felt like our stretch of the river had been invaded. Our house sat directly between the dredging zone and the processing facility.

By late August, the barges had moved so close that one was anchored just yards from our dock. We now lived at the epicenter of the operation. The time we dreaded had arrived.

Aside from limited paddling, the project disrupted our lives far less than expected. The noise was quieter than we had feared and the lights less obtrusive. At night, the river transformed into a dazzling light show, the glowing barges casting shimmering reflections on the water. When the excavator worked only yards from our dock, I enjoyed sitting there, watching the nighttime operations up close.

In the months and years leading up to this, I imagined with trepidation what would happen when the dredging arrived. I wondered if it would even be safe to stay in our home and briefly considered alternatives. However, a viable one never surfaced.

But when the time came, I chose to engage rather than resist. I educated myself, tracked the data, and embraced the rare opportunity to witness a historic environmental cleanup firsthand. Since I could neither control anything about the project nor leave for the summer, I focused on what I *could* control: my attitude and inner peacefulness.

I could spend the season in frustration and resistance. Or I could reach for something better: curiosity, fascination, creative inspiration. I documented the process through writing and photography, making the most of a situation I had dreaded.

In time, the barges disappeared. The river quieted. Our sunrise view was restored. We could kayak freely once more. Missing a season of paddling was a small sacrifice in the river's long journey of renewal.

Once again, the river taught me to move with the current rather than get caught in an eddy of worry. So often, what we fear never comes to pass. And even when it does, we can trust that we have the inner and outer resources to meet it.

Dredging Meets Patrick Cottonwood

In both my Nature Photography and Mindfulness in Nature classes, I recommend the practice of befriending a tree with curiosity and attentiveness. It involves

- ❖ observing the tree as often as possible, at different times of day and throughout the seasons

- ❖ noticing how the light changes

- ❖ zooming in and out to take in both the whole and the details

- ❖ suspending your knowledge base temporarily and experiencing the tree with your senses rather than your mind.

Patrick Cottonwood is my Hudson River tree friend. I photographed him extensively while floating in my kayak beneath the canopy of one of his low-hanging branches. Dazzled by the seasonal transformations he underwent, I had shared my awe with my kindergarten students. However, a year after I befriended him, something happened that changed our relationship.

In the spring of 2013, our section of the river was being prepared for dredging. I noticed that many of the trees lining the opposite riverbank had been marked with fluorescent orange paint—targets for trimming or removal, to make room for the dredging machinery. I was relieved to see Patrick wasn't marked.

Then, one day on my drive home, I saw an orange barrier around him. The tree that had stood beside him, marked for removal, was gone. Only a stump remained.

That evening, Jack and I paddled out to photograph the marked trees one last time. Aside from those involved in the project, we were likely the only ones who realized how many trees would be lost. The orange dots were not visible from the road. They could only be seen up close, from the slow-moving perspective of the river.

As we paddled, birds perched in the marked trees, singing. It was heartbreaking to think of all the wildlife that would be displaced.

From the water, Patrick looked like a prisoner of war, cordoned off. Though not marked for removal, he would lose limbs. The sight was a battlefield, with so many marked trees standing defenseless on the front lines, about to lose their lives without any say in the matter.

On my way home the next day, I stopped to check on Patrick. The tree cutters had been at work. I arrived just as they were finishing, hauling away pieces of Patrick on a barge, en route to a landfill. From the roadside, I could see two of Patrick's major branches had been removed, including the low-hanging limbs I had loved to photograph and float beneath.

My heart was heavy, but I wasn't upset with the workers. They were doing their jobs, providing for themselves and their families. If they hadn't done it, someone else would have. I trusted that those involved in the project believed they were serving the greater good, and that the sacrifices in the natural world would be worth it in the long run and would cause less harm than leaving the toxins buried in the riverbed.

That evening, I couldn't bear to paddle out and experience the changes from my kayak. Instead, I approached Patrick from the road and rested my hand on his bark. There is growing scientific evidence that trees are highly responsive to their environment. They can detect light, gravity, moisture, and chemical signals from other plants. Through their roots and symbiotic fungal networks, they exchange nutrients and information, communicating in ways we are only beginning to understand. While their perception differs from ours, trees are deeply attuned to the world around them. In addition to being connected with other trees, I liked to believe Patrick somehow sensed he was seen and appreciated by a human.

The next day when the dredging was paused, I took my kayak out to survey the aftermath. Tree stumps lined the shore. All the trees that once provided shade and privacy were gone. The landscape was entirely changed.

Until that paddle, I hadn't known the exact locations of the PCB hot spots that were awaiting dredging. But the stumps provided a map. The hot spots ran the entire length of my route on the opposite shore and a short stretch on our side of the river. Upon returning home, I checked a map from the Environmental Protection Agency. Sure enough, the pattern of stumps matched the EPA's map exactly.

My relationship with Patrick changed after he lost his low branches. He became the kind of friend I greeted in passing rather than lingered with in intimate conversation. He still towered over the river, but I experienced him differently: more as a whole than in the details I once cherished.

Yet Patrick still holds a special place in my heart. When you take the time to truly know a living being—to witness and understand it deeply—love and care naturally follow. The delights of observing the details of Patrick's seasonal changes and experiencing the sunlight passing through the leaves of his low-lying branches are in the past. That is the nature of things. All conditions in life are impermanent.

Patrick stood tall overlooking the river long before PCBs were dumped into the water, and he remains standing now. More than a decade later, the wound where his lower limb was amputated has scarred over. Once raw and tragic, it is now barely noticeable.

As sad as I was when Patrick lost his limbs, today he looks strong and healthy. He has survived harsh years and remains deeply rooted, a silent teacher of resilience, impermanence, and taking the long view. And what we can't see beneath the ground is how Patrick remains connected to the other trees. Though he may appear separate and alone, he never was.

Neither are we.

Patrick before trimming   *Patrick after trimming*

Don't-Know Mind

Although cleaning up a polluted river might sound like an obvious solution, the Hudson River dredging project was hotly debated and closely watched worldwide. I first encountered the pro-dredging environmentalist argument in 2001 at the Clearwater Festival (Great Hudson River Revival), where Jack's band performed for several years. Founded in 1966 by Toshi Seeger and her husband, folk singer Pete Seeger, the festival featured prominent signs demanding that General Electric (GE) clean up the mess it had made in the Hudson.

It wasn't until 2008, when we moved to the banks of the river, that I encountered opposing viewpoints. Many local residents believed the Hudson would heal itself naturally if left undisturbed. Wildlife, including bald eagles, had returned, and they feared dredging would stir up toxins, turning the river into a toxic stew. However, according to a Clearwater fact sheet, the river wasn't "cleaning itself." [7]

In 1976, the Upper Hudson between Hudson Falls and the Troy dam was closed to fishing because the fish were severely contaminated with PCBs. When sportfishing was reopened in 1995, it was on a catch-and-release basis only. Yet restrictions didn't stop people from eating contaminated fish if they chose to. The EPA's long-term goal was that, after more than fifty years of post-dredging natural recovery, fish from the Hudson could be consumed safely once a week. [6]

The controversy continues today. The EPA maintains that PCB levels have declined significantly as expected, while environmental organizations like Riverkeeper argue that data shows otherwise, raising concerns about health risks to those who eat the fish.[8]

For local residents, the issue was deeply personal. The pro-dredging stance, by contrast, tended to take a long-term, ecological view. Even within the pro-dredging camp, however, opinions and politics varied.

Since the issue was so complex, and I am not a scientist, I never felt comfortable taking a firm side. Instead, I adopted the Zen practice of *don't-know mind*: being aware of our views while not clinging to them, engaging with a subject openly and inquisitively without needing to be right, and resting in uncertainty. Don't-know mind acknowledges that every issue has multiple perspectives and keeps us receptive to possibilities we might not yet see. It allows us to pay attention and see clearly, without blinders.

The truth is, despite our opinions and personal preferences, nobody knows for certain whether the dredging ultimately will be deemed successful.

I reasoned that any personal inconveniences from the dredging would be trivial if the project truly improved the river's health in the long run. The Hudson doesn't just run through eastern New York; it runs through generations. When I sat on the dock and listened deeply, I sensed that removing the PCBs would serve the river's future, even if full restoration doesn't happen in my lifetime. I liked to imagine future generations enjoying a clean Hudson. Witnessing migratory birds like great blue herons and egrets feasting on contaminated fish reminded me that there are no real boundaries to the pollution.

I listened to community voices without passing judgment or allowing their opinions to determine mine. One day, as dredging began in our area, I visited a local park and overheard an older man exclaim, "It's disgusting!" The hum of a motor in the background told me dredging was underway near the lock adjacent to the park.

We struck up a conversation. He was dismayed by how sloppy the excavator looked emerging from the water. He didn't trust that it was containing the PCBs and feared resuspension: a widespread concern among locals. He pointed out that wildlife had returned in recent years and questioned why anyone would think it wise to disturb the settled toxins.

I walked over to the lock to take photos. The excavator had paused, and I watched the barges move around. A man approached and asked if I was familiar with the dredging project. As we spoke, I learned he was organizing an upcoming triathlon near the dredging site. Like me, he had educated himself about PCBs, and as his knowledge grew, his fears lessened. There was a big difference between blindly accepting PR messaging, whether for or against dredging, and educating oneself through research and talking with experts.

I arrived at the dredging site not only as a writer and photographer bearing witness but also as a resident about to have dredging barges in front of my home. I wanted to observe the process firsthand, to understand what to expect. Sitting at a picnic table near the operation, I found myself engrossed and wondered how history would judge this project. Would it be a net positive? Perhaps. But true clarity would take time. Those of us alive now are merely witnesses to one chapter of the river's story.

This reminds me of the parable often attributed to Taoist or Zen tradition, of the farmer whose only horse ran away. The neighbors lamented his misfortune, to which the farmer simply replied, "Maybe."

Then the horse returned, bringing another horse. "What good luck!" the neighbors exclaimed.

"Maybe," the farmer said.

Then his son broke his leg riding the new horse. "What bad luck!" the neighbors said.

"Maybe," replied the farmer.

When soldiers came to conscript young men for war, they passed over the injured son. "What good luck!" the neighbors exclaimed.

"Maybe," said the farmer.

And so the story goes on.

Later that day, as I recorded a video at the dredging site, a woman approached and asked what was happening. Someone replied, "Dredging," and her jaw dropped. She was a swimmer in the upcoming triathlon.

I understood her reaction. The New York State Department of Health advised against swallowing river water and recommended showering after physical contact with it to reduce exposure to bacteria and contaminants. That year, our area was designated a No-Swim Zone. Though I assumed the triathlon course lay outside it, how close was too close? That was a personal decision, best made through careful, unbiased research and trusting one's gut.

My understanding was that the primary risks of PCB exposure come from eating contaminated fish, having contact with sediment, and inhaling contaminated dust. Despite being an avid kayaker on the Upper Hudson, I had always taken a conservative approach to physical contact with the water; that felt right to me. But if others chose differently, that was their decision to make, not mine to judge.

Listening to people's stories at the dredging site felt a little like group therapy. Everyone I met had a connection to the river, and that bond connected us all. The diversity of perspectives painted a rich, complex portrait of how the Hudson shapes people's lives. I wished the animals could tell their stories, too!

I don't know what the river's health will be in the future. And as much as I love the river, I must be okay with the uncertainty. So many variables will shape its fate. Will environmental protections hold? Who knows?

My deep hope is that the dredging will benefit generations to come, and that people and corporations will stop treating our rivers, oceans, and waterways as dumping grounds. As I have learned from observing the Hudson's wildlife, water connects us all. Contaminated fish are canaries in a coal mine, and our survival depends on the quality of the water and air we share.

DREDGING THE DEPTHS

The summer of 2013 was a summer of dredging, both on the river and within myself. For months, I watched from my home as enormous excavators churned up the riverbed, removing hot spot after hot spot of sediment contaminated with PCBs. The process was methodical and relentless. Massive barges carried the toxic muck away, hauling it upriver to be loaded onto trains bound for a landfill across the country specifically designed to handle hazardous waste.

The parallels were impossible to ignore. While the river was being dredged, I was dredging up my own layers of toxicity: old wounds, ingrained habits, and deeply rooted patterns that had long settled in me. Just as the machines pulled up pollutants buried for decades, my circumstances were pulling up painful memories and strong emotions. The biggest challenge I faced was boundaries. I'd always struggled with them. Saying no, standing my ground, and protecting my own space all felt impossibly daunting.

I often felt uniquely flawed. *What's wrong with me? Why is this so hard?* But I've learned not to believe every thought that arises. Meeting thoughts with mindfulness allowed me to question them, take a deeper look, and realize that my struggle wasn't a personal failing. It was a pattern handed down to me. My parents and grandparents had modeled friendliness above all else. People-pleasing was in my blood, a habit energy so strong it felt impossible to undo.

That summer, I found myself in a situation in which my gentle nature was being taken advantage of, and boundaries I didn't know how to hold were being trampled upon. I believed that kindness and compassion were spiritual virtues but didn't understand at the time the difference between immature and wise compassion. Even my beliefs about compassion needed to be brought into the light.

The river had become my refuge. Paddling in my kayak gave me solace, perspective, and strength. But that, too, was taken away. The dredging made the river inaccessible six days a week. Constant traffic from barges and tugboats kept the surface in motion and lacking the calm, reflective quality I found so soothing. I felt powerless against forces much bigger than myself, just as I felt powerless in my struggle to hold firm against overbearing personalities in my life.

But something kept drawing me to the dock at night, watching the dredging crew at work.

We still don't know whether the Hudson River Superfund cleanup will go down in history as a success or a failure. Maybe it would have been better to leave those toxins buried, undisturbed, rather than risk stirring them up. Maybe the effort would never fully cleanse the river. But even so, I couldn't help but feel a sense of hope as I watched the work being done—the determination to remove what did not belong, to create conditions for the river ecosystem to thrive.

A river can be a metaphor for life itself.

We all carry toxins in the form of negative beliefs, sabotaging patterns, and limiting stories that trace back to earlier experiences and, perhaps, even generations. Sometimes they settle quietly at the bottom, out of sight but still there. And sometimes life dredges them up, making everything feel messier, murkier, and more painful before it gets better. Seeing our patterns and beliefs clearly is the first step in transforming them, and that can't be done if they remain buried and unconscious. If we take a good, honest look at what is coming up and keep doing the work, clearing out what doesn't serve us, we create a favorable environment for greater well-being.

And we can develop self-compassion for whatever comes up. Instead of shipping away the unhealthy patterns, we can make our hearts and minds vast enough to hold and transmute them. Or offer them to the earth, to compost into new, healthy growth. The opportunity is to make sure the old, unhealthy stuff won't be allowed to resettle in the same way.

For a time, the river is disrupted. The water runs dark with sediment. But in the end, if the effort is sustained, it has the potential to become cleaner, healthier, and more vibrant than before.

The same is true for us.

RIVER ANCESTORS

A long the riverbank, spring and summer unfold in a shifting
parade of colors, as one kind of flower after another steps
into the spotlight before making way for the next. The parade
begins with the daisies, which give way to lilies-of-the-valley, red
columbines, forget-me-nots, black-eyed Susans, orange day lilies,
purple chicory, fuchsia thistle, Queen Anne's lace, and many
others. The flowers along the shore remind me of those who
lived here before us and the larger life rhythms we ourselves are
part of.

We are the current residents of a house built roughly 200
years ago, a home that has seen many inhabitants come and go.
When I take in the river landscape, I sometimes think of the
different generations of families and individuals who have lived
and loved within these walls and who have gazed upon the river
from this same vantage point. The view from my bedroom
window is the same view they once saw. Like the flowers, each
generation becomes part of the landscape. No life form lasts
forever. Each is replaced in turn. We are part of this ongoing
chain.

The land on which the house sits has witnessed much history:
the seasonal camps of Native peoples long ago, the turbulence
of the French and Indian Wars, the battles of the Revolutionary
War, the opening of the Champlain Canal in 1823 that brought
prosperity to the region, and the eventual decline of the industrial era.

The river that flows past our house was essential to the lives
of the Mohicans who once dwelled on these banks and fished
in these waters, and to the Mohawks, who eventually displaced

them as part of the broader tides of conflict and migration long before European settlers arrived.

And it has borne different names, in different languages, long before it was named for the early seventeenth century English explorer, Henry Hudson. Italian-born explorer Giovanni da Verrazzano, sailing in service of France, called it River of the Steep Hills. It was also known as *Noordt Rivier* (North River) by the Dutch, *Muhheakantuck* (river that flows both ways) by the Mohican people, and *Mohicanhitheck* (river of the Mohegans) by the Lenni-Lenape people. It was known by many other names, as well. Whatever name it was given, the river was integral to the lives of many generations of humans.[9]

Through centuries of change—colonial wars, pioneer settlements, turning point of the Revolutionary War, the rise of the canal era, and the coming of the railroad—the river remained a lifeline for food, transport, commerce, and connection. With the opening of the Erie and Champlain canals, both meeting the Hudson at Waterford, the river became the economic backbone of New York State, transporting goods and people between New York City and the Great Lakes, Vermont, and Canada.

One Fourth of July, my son, Cianan, and I sat on the dock listening to the booming fireworks in the distance and watching a spectacular display of heat lightning moving slowly south along the river. The heat lightning continued long after the fireworks had ended, although the night was still punctuated now and then by the sudden bangs of private celebrations. A campfire glowed softly across the water on the opposite shore. The sights and sounds felt timeless.

Taking in the night's sounds and sights, I think of those who sat in this same spot amid the intense sounds of conflict centuries ago. It is easy to imagine the echo of cannons across the river during the Revolutionary War or the sleepless vigilance of scouts and settlers. Sometimes, I've paddled at night, imagining others navigating the river long ago under cover of darkness, perhaps hoping not to be seen by enemies.

Next to our house is a shed that is said to have served as part of a Revolutionary War field hospital. When I walk around the yard at night and all is quiet but for the crickets, I can feel its history—and feel my own footsteps becoming part of it.

The flowers, too, have their daily rhythms of opening and closing, along with their graceful life cycles of growing and dissolving. A year's unfolding includes so many different kinds of blooms, almost like notes played in a musical composition. Everything blooms in its own time and drops its seeds so the whole dance can continue. I find great comfort in being part of these natural rhythms and feel blessed to be here now.

Before living in this house, I didn't think much about previous inhabitants of the places I lived. But here, my connection with the land is so strong, and the pull of history is almost inescapable. The land itself invites a deep reverence for those who came before.

Years ago, I became absorbed in the book, *Early Days in Eastern Saratoga County* by Grace VanDerwerker (originally published as a series of pamphlets beginning in 1928).[10] I was riveted by accounts of incidents that took place in our home, our yard, and our river community long ago.

The VanDerwerker book includes an account of emergency surgery performed in our house in the 1870s following a sawmill accident across the river. The accident victim lived in the house. I found him listed in the 1880 census, along with the other members of the household. I had hoped to locate their graves or any other information about them, but my searches came up empty. I also learned that bricks were manufactured on the hill behind our house in the late 1860s, which explains why we have found bricks buried in the ground.

Locating where events from long ago took place often depends heavily on descriptions of landmarks. Roads, town names, and boundaries have changed so much over the centuries that it is difficult to pinpoint specific addresses. But the river still ran through.

I often think about the intimacy we have with our ancestors. There are blood ancestors with whom we share genetic code, cultural traditions, and family values. And there are land ancestors, who lived on the same ground, woke up inside the same walls, and looked out at the same view.

Even though I am not a native of this town and may not remain here forever, I feel a deep sense of belonging to the ongoing story of this place. I'm curious about those who came before me.

Who walked up these stairs?
Who slept in these bedrooms?
Who died here?
If there were children, where did they play?
Were they happy?
What were their dreams, their joys, their hardships?
What was their relationship with the river like?

One evening, as I was driving home, a magnificent rainbow stretched across the sky. When I passed a local cemetery, I noticed the rainbow arching vividly behind it and pulled over to take some photos. When I got home and took a closer look at the images, I became intrigued by the names on the tombstones. That may have been the moment my interest in the early settlers was truly ignited.

One stormy night, I sat alone reading the VanDerwerker book as a fierce thunderstorm blew in. Lightning and hail hammered the roof. I was reading about the fear the early settlers lived with, particularly the fear of attacks by the Mohawks. I could almost feel their fear myself.

The next day, I took the book up to the old cemetery on the hill, where soldiers of five different wars are buried, and spent hours reading names from the gravestones and looking them up in the book's index. I had already read most of the stories and felt a thrill of recognition stumbling across the graves of those whose lives and dramas I had come to know.

The names and stories came alive there among the tombstones. I knew the gossip: who was highly respected, who were the doctors, the deacons, the soldiers, even who had been murdered. Somehow, I felt at home among all these personalities, as if I, too, am part of the long story of this land through which the river flows.

While I am fortunate not to live in a time of war here on the river (and hope that will continue), I did witness a major historical event: the monumental PCBs dredging of the Hudson River. I photographed it extensively as it unfolded around me. Perhaps someday, some of my photographs will become part of local historical records and help future generations picture what life was like here along the river in the early twenty-first century.

Who knows what kinds of imprints we leave on the land and water that hold our stories? Some part of us remains wherever we have lived and loved deeply. And so, I will always be part of this river.

In the end, the river carries us all—our stories, our dreams, our dramas—toward the endless sea of time.

Lewis Pugh's
Historic Hudson River Swim

The river sings many songs to those willing to listen. Sometimes it's a song of impermanence, sometimes of surprise or awe. It can be a song of history, of interconnection, or even uncertainty. You never know what will come down the river from moment to moment.

In the summer of 2018 while kayaking, I spotted a curious boat heading toward me, unlike anything I'd ever seen. It turned out to be a rustic houseboat, a loose replica of a shantyboat, that was part of Wes Modes' project, *A Secret History of American River People*.[11] The boat, built from recycled materials, was collecting stories from communities along the river. It was a remarkable sight and a fascinating story in itself. That day, the river sang a song of wonder and reminded me of the value of being prepared—for I encountered the story boat without a camera.

Usually, what comes down the river is unexpected: wildlife sightings, like the occasional swan or loon. Sometimes, though, you get advance notice. In the summer of 2023, I caught sight of a fleet of kayaks in celebration of the 200th anniversary of the Champlain Canal. It was like a river parade, and I couldn't resist photographing the vibrant colors and positive, contagious energy.

Soon after, I learned that Lewis Pugh, ocean advocate and British-South African endurance swimmer extraordinaire, would be swimming the entire 315-mile length of the Hudson River from mid-August to mid-September. He planned to arrive in

New York City in time for the United Nations General Assembly Week, Climate Week NYC 2023, and the U.N. Secretary General's Climate Ambition Summit.

Pugh has completed incredible endurance swims across the globe, including the North Pole and Mount Everest's glacial lake. He was the first to swim the length of the British Channel and complete long-distance swims in all five oceans. His awe-inspiring achievements are undertaken to draw attention to fragile ecosystems. As the United Nations Patron of the Oceans, he earned recognition as *National Geographic*'s 2014 Adventurer of the Year.

When I learned that Pugh would be swimming the Hudson, I didn't want to miss it. His mission was to highlight the interdependence of river and ocean health and promote the restoration and protection of our rivers. Earlier that month, I had completed my own yearlong river photography project and felt a special kinship with anyone undertaking a river-based endeavor.

The day Pugh swam through our area, I went kayaking, hoping to catch a glimpse of him. Two hours passed without a sign, and I became completely absorbed in watching a great white egret. Had I missed him, or was he running behind schedule? I paddled back home and almost immediately after entering the house saw a bright green double kayak alongside a swimmer heading down the middle of the river. It was him!

I bolted to the riverside with my camera and cheered him on. He swam on the other side of the kayak, so I couldn't get a good shot from my spot on the bank. Feeling like a paddling paparazzi, I jumped into my own kayak for a better view. After a few minutes, I paddled back home, then drove to a park further down the road, where he was headed.

At the park, a small group of supporters gathered on the dock just before the lock, where we were told Pugh would exit the water for a lunchtime meet-and-greet. Soon, we spotted the green kayak in the distance, and excitement rippled through the crowd.

Pugh made his way to the pavilion, sat down to eat, and I seized the chance to talk with him. When I introduced myself, he asked if I was from the press. "No," I said, "I'm from the river!" I told him about my river project, which was the opposite of his; I stayed in one spot for a whole year photographing river sunrises, while he was navigating the entire length of the river. As someone deeply in love with the river, I expressed my gratitude for his efforts to advocate for both rivers and oceans.

He wondered why the beautiful park was so quiet, remarking that in England, there would be lots of people enjoying it.

One of the team members kayaking alongside him asked if I had seen the bald eagle near the dam when I was in my kayak. I hadn't— because I'd been focused on them. However, I'd photographed their sighting of the eagle.

Soon, more locals gathered in the pavilion for an engaging hourlong conversation. We discussed Alfred Lansing's adventure book, *Endurance: Shackleton's Incredible Voyage*[12], Pugh's South Georgia swim, and the challenges of reaching remote places. Local history also came up, including the origin of Hudson Crossing Park's name and a nearby house still bearing cannonballs in the walls from the Revolutionary War. We also talked about the PCBs dredging and the return of river wildlife like bald eagles, osprey, and herons.

Here we were, a small group of Americans discussing the Revolutionary War at a site where it had actually taken place, with a British swimmer passing through, advocating for the health of oceans and rivers that connect and sustain all life. In that brief meeting, local history intersected with a much larger global story.

I found Pugh to be quietly well-spoken, with a calm, centered presence and a characteristic British sense of humor. As the conversation continued, I couldn't help but reflect on how many stories he must hear as he stops in river communities along his route, like the story boat from five years prior.

Over the next few days, I tried to catch up with Pugh again but each time arrived just a few minutes too late. Since I couldn't get more pictures of him, the ones taken between our house and the park had to suffice. The one that meant the most to me was of him swimming past the former PCBs processing site. Ten years prior, this spot had been the epicenter of the Superfund dredging project, with huge barges hauling contaminated soil from the riverbed. But now, Pugh was swimming for the health of our rivers, and photographing him in that spot was deeply symbolic to me.

To express what I saw in my mind's eye as he swam through this spot, I created a composite of that image and one I had taken in the same spot during the dredging years. The resulting image expressed why Pugh decided to swim the Hudson: as a symbol of environmental progress and hope for rivers world-wide.

I followed his daily progress on his website and learned a lot about the river along the way. His endeavor put the quiet stretch of river I know so well into a much greater context.

Lewis Pugh successfully completed his swim at Battery Park in New York City—a far cry from the small, upstate river communities he passed through earlier in his journey. His swim through our area was incredibly inspiring, sparking a renewed desire to explore more of the river that is so dear to me. I am truly grateful to have met this extraordinary human being and wonder how his journey impacted the minds and hearts of others up and down the river.

I imagine it would be equally compelling to hear stories from the different river communities, the questions Pugh was asked, and the answers he gave, as he made his way from the Adirondack High Peaks region to New York City. Given the chance to talk with him again, I would ask him what goes through his mind as he swims and what his attention is like. I've wondered about that ever since meeting him. That would be a very different conversation indeed.

FAST BOATS

The river is my peaceful place. But for years, one thing disturbed my river bliss more than anything else: fast boats.

When I started meditating nearly forty years ago, my expectations were lofty. I hoped to see visions, experience altered states of consciousness, receive special knowledge—*and* calm my nervous system. But after a whole lot of living, my reasons for meditating have become simpler and more practical. Mindfulness enriches my daily life in ways both small and profound.

Here's an example: In the early years, when a yacht or motorboat sped past my kayak, I'd seethe with frustration. The turbulence on the water mirrored the disturbance in my mind. I'd judge the boaters as selfish, and my agitation would linger, tinged with resentment over their wealth and privilege. "Selfish, rich people who think they own the river!" I'd mutter under my breath.

That was the story in my head. Eventually, I'd let it go . . . until the next boat sped by. Truth be told, beneath my frustration was fear. I worried the waves would capsize my kayak. Once, a wave of Hudson River water hit me square in the face, and I didn't want that to happen again. As much as I love the river, I do my best to avoid direct physical contact with it, even after the dredging.

Over the years, as my mindfulness practice deepened both on the meditation cushion and in daily life, my attitude toward the fast boats changed. I became less reactive.

You never know what will happen on the river. I can't control how boaters will behave. Some slow down when they approach a kayak. Others don't.

However, there is a lot I *can* control. I can go on the river when boat traffic is lighter. I can secure my belongings in waterproof containers tethered to my kayak. To keep my distance, I can stay on the side of the river that is furthest from the navigation zone. It's not my preferred side, but what a gift it is to have a river in front of my house in the first place. And the waves? When you let go of fear, they can be fun to bounce around on.

More importantly, I can observe my self-talk and step out of the stories my mind manufactures about boaters, focusing instead on staying in the here and now. In the past, after a boat sped by, I carried that frustration down the river with me. The story fueled my emotions, keeping me stuck in suffering. Maybe I noticed some beauty around me, but I wasn't fully present.

Here is a common scenario: A boat barrels toward me. I make the "slow-down" gesture with my hand. The helmsman waves but doesn't slow down. One even turned around and passed by again, making a bucking motion that generated stronger waves. Was it in response to my disapproval? Were they just having fun, oblivious to how their wake affected kayakers? I'll never know . . . and it's not my business. My business is generating an inner steadiness and safely navigating the waves.

When stories arise, I can question them: *Am I sure?* Are there other explanations besides selfishness and disregard? Of course there are. Maybe they've never been kayaking and don't realize how their wake affects small boats. Maybe they're in a hurry. Maybe they're simply enjoying the ride and not paying attention, and it's not personal. Maybe they can't see my kayak. Maybe they're not being intentionally rude, and my reaction says more about me than about them.

Our experience on the river is shaped by what we carry within us, often without realizing it. So, when I find myself easily perturbed by fast boaters, that reaction can be a mindfulness bell that cues honest and compassionate self-reflection. Am I feeling powerless elsewhere in life? If so, how might I set myself free? Taking responsibility for our own patterns and reactions is an empowering shift.

Feeling angry at the boaters never hurt them; it only hurt me. It doesn't serve me to make up stories about their character or motives. I can do my best to control what is within my sphere of control, then ride the waves with as much awareness and skill as possible.

The boats on the river haven't changed. But I have. Now, when a yacht comes barreling down the river, it cues me to open my mindfulness toolbox. I remind myself: This is not my private river. The boats have as much right to be here as I do. I don't expect them to slow down. I drop resistance and allow the experience to be exactly as it is. I trust in my ability to navigate whatever turbulence arises. If the boat slows down, wonderful—how considerate! But I don't need them to. Either way, I trust myself to handle the waves. After all, I have a lot of experience in doing so.

I understand there are risks associated with being on the river. Every time I go out in my kayak, I choose to assume those risks over staying on the sidelines—the riverbank.

If the word "wealthy" slips in with a negative connotation, it's a mindfulness bell alerting me to an abundance block. I take notice and breathe. I put some spaciousness around the thought and feel grateful and prosperous for my easy, daily access to the river. To counter the rich boater stereotype, I remember Paul, my late cousin from British Columbia, who loved the water and spent a lot of time on a sixty-eight-foot yacht. Paul was one of my favorite people in the world. I've even trained my mind to think, "Hello, Paul!" when a yacht passes by, instead of spiraling into negativity. Sometimes, I'll look back and see a Canadian flag flapping on the boat, which feels like Paul replying, "Hello, cuz!"

I might even send lovingkindness in the boat's direction: *May you be well. May you be safe. May you live with ease.* Ahhh, that's better. Same situation. Totally different response. A little awareness makes a big difference. Awareness + spaciousness + better go-to thoughts = GAME CHANGER. Awareness opens the door to transformation.

It makes a difference to cultivate equanimity, not just toward boaters who create turbulence, but toward people who aren't looking out for me and toward bugs buzzing around me. These things are part of life. If we go out on the river, chances are we will encounter waves. We're grateful when warm weather arrives, but it awakens the flying insects. Unsatisfactoriness is part of life. But we can prepare ourselves, so life's inevitable waves don't disturb our peace of mind so much. We can cultivate equanimity and a deep aspiration to free ourselves from suffering.

The goal is not to eliminate every difficult person, challenging circumstance, or disappointment. It is to cultivate inner peace despite them. That is true freedom.

The river is a fitting metaphor for life. Turbulence and things not going your way are inevitable. But it is easier to ride the waves when you can catch and release thoughts that don't serve. You accept the waves as part of this human life and maybe even find joy in the ride.

Ultimately, it's about choosing not to let the waves, the boaters, or the world's turbulence upset your peace. You can't always change the external world, but you can choose how you respond. You can stop making yourself miserable, sending unpleasant waves of energy into the world. And you can choose, repeatedly, to come back to presence and meet the moment with greater steadiness and skill.

What Do You See?

There is a small spot on the riverside nearby just large enough for a small family or a few friends to enjoy the water and launch their kayaks. It gets a lot of use, which is great. However, people often leave behind their trash.

One day, as I paddled past, I felt disheartened and disgusted by the sight of garbage piling up. It fit into a familiar narrative of selfishness that had been grating on me during the COVID shutdown. And so, of course, that is what I saw: entitlement, irresponsibility, a lack of care for others and for the earth.

I paddled away, stewing in frustration, feeling separate from —and somehow better than—the people who had left their trash behind. But something about that feeling didn't sit right. How far down the river was I willing to carry this indignation?

One of the gifts of a regular meditation practice is the ability to notice when the mind is heading into dark and divisive places. Awareness opens a field of spaciousness where the heart can step in and speak. It became clear that, just as people could do better at cleaning up after themselves, I could do better than judging them. So, I paddled forward with a simple prayer in my heart:

> *May I and all beings be free from the suffering and ignorance that cause harm.*
> *May I and all beings be free from the suffering and ignorance that close the heart.*

That felt better. I was back in connection with my wise heart and with other human beings.

Our struggles and the demons we wrestle with are universal, even if they take different forms. We get activated, addicted, distracted, stuck. We fall short, miss the mark, make mistakes. This is the human condition.

One of the biggest lessons I've learned is that when we stop blaming and making others wrong, and instead examine our own reactions, we reclaim our power. Because the only person we can change is . . . you know who. When we shift the way we see something, new possibilities arise.

If we explore a little deeper, we will likely find that beneath anger, judgment, and indignation, there is often some kind of caring. The light of love, kindness, and compassion wants to shine forth, but the ego obstructs it when things aren't the way it thinks they should be.

That caring in me sparked ideas. I could put up a simple sign inviting people to enjoy the spot while remembering to carry out their trash. Stash a few bags for those who hadn't thought to bring their own. Or put on gloves and clean it up myself. Instead of seeing another reason to disconnect, I could see an opportunity to be of service and part of a solution.

The great news is that before I had the chance to act, someone else did! The next time I paddled by, the spot had been cleaned. Another caring heart had stepped in.

Since then, I have paddled by the little riverside spot countless times and reflected on how it is connected with all the things we resist in the world, in our lives, and in ourselves. Could those, too, be invitations to shine more light? Litter. Shame. Judgment. The impulse to believe I am right, and you are wrong. Regrets and mistakes. Even fear.

What do you see when you come across a heap of garbage by the roadside? When you look in the mirror? When you take in the news? When you engage with someone who sees the world differently than you do?

Can we learn to hold what we reject in a more spacious way, that allows for insight and caring to arise? Can we include it in our circle of lovingkindness, so it can awaken our natural wisdom and compassion instead of keeping us rigid and stuck?

Yes, we can. It all depends on how we look at it. Held the right way, the demons we wrestle become allies that help us to evolve. To love better.

DIFFERENT VIEWS

From our spot on the west bank of the river, we are treated to glorious sunrises and, on occasion, stunning sunsets.

One evening, puffy white clouds, clearly reflected in the calm water, drew me into my kayak. I almost didn't bring my camera. Leaving the house, I assured myself the phone camera would suffice. I wanted to travel lightly, focusing on paddling, not photography. But in a moment of waiting for traffic to pass before crossing the road, intuition nudged me to go back inside and get my camera. Fortunately, I listened to that voice, and forty-five minutes later, I was floating on a river of awe. The clouds had transformed into cotton-candy pink as the sun sank toward the horizon, creating a breathtaking scene. Once again, I was reminded of how a simple "sacred pause" can allow intuition, inspiration, and wisdom to emerge: things often missed when we are on autopilot or lost in thought.

As I paddled to the other side of the river, the clouds that had beckoned me there were no longer visible. People living on the east bank wouldn't even have known the clouds had been there. From that side of the river, I could see a large cloud hovering over our house, backlit by the setting sun and glowing with an otherworldly light. It reminded me of the saying: *Every cloud has a silver lining.*

From our house, nestled in the river valley at the bottom of a hill, we would not have seen *that* cloud. Similarly, we rarely get to experience more than a faint hint of the breathtaking sunsets that happen on the hilltops above us, visible only from the other side of the river.

While floating in my kayak, I thought about how our view of the world is shaped by where we "live," both literally and figuratively. Which way we face, what portion of the sky we see, and where we are situated all influence our perspective. Residents of one side of the river might have a very different experience of the landscape, the cycles of day and night, or even the quality of light, compared to those across the river or up on a hill in either direction. Some may be accustomed to sunsets rather than sunrises or enjoy longer stretches of daylight than we do at the bottom of the hill.

It's not just about the sky. On one side of the river, property might be more prone to flooding, and people may pay more for flood insurance or avoid it entirely and feel more anxious during weather events. Numerous factors shape our experiences, though we might not think to consider the experiences of others if they don't affect us and aren't on our radar.

We often have no idea what is visible to those on the other side of the river. To adopt a wider perspective, we must sometimes step into someone else's shoes—or kayak, or house—and see the world from their vantage point. Then, we might truly grasp what it looks like from where they stand.

When I was teaching kindergarten, I loved experiencing the sunrise from my home on one side of the river and enjoying the sunset from the other side, on my way home from work. It was like experiencing two entirely different points of view.

River Neighbors

The sight of the clouds over the river reminded me of a time when a public figure enrolled in one of my nature photography courses. It was a year into the COVID pandemic, and people were understandably more sensitive and tense. I wondered if this person's presence would be distracting for some.

The universe had pitched me an invitation to grow beyond my comfort zone, and it ended up being a transformative experience. While I had time to prepare, the participants did not. I wanted to skillfully manage whatever dynamics might arise and connect with everyone as human beings, not public personas.

During our first session, after covering some technical content, I shifted focus to the inner dimensions of photography, which is where the magic is for me. I spoke about how nature photography serves as a bridge, not only connecting us to the natural world but also to each other.

I said that I know many of our river neighbors on both sides of our section of the river, and though we may not all share the same worldview, our mutual appreciation for the river unites us. We talk affectionately about the bald eagles, herons, loons, and swans that call the river home, and we commiserate about the noise from the bridge. Often, a neighbor will send me a message if they see something worth photographing.

This shared experience of life on the river connects us. And it's not just specific to the Hudson River; I have found a similar bond with those who have lived near any river. There is a universal connection among "river people."

I appreciate when my river neighbors share their pictures because they help me see what I might have missed, whether it's a view of the sky or the fog from their perspective. Through their love for the river, their goodness shines, and I can appreciate their inner light, even if we have opposing views. It's a reminder that our views are only a small part of who we are. Our views and opinions, no matter how strongly held, are not our essence.

I shared with the class that, beneath our differences, everyone was drawn to the nature photography course because of some kind of caring, longing, or appreciation. No matter how differently my river neighbors or course participants relate to current events, I aim to look deeper, for our common humanity. Beneath the surface, we all share some kind of caring, or perhaps wounding, that connects us.

Henry Wadsworth Longfellow once wrote:

> *If we could read the secret history of our enemies, we should find in each [person's] life sorrow and suffering enough to disarm all hostility.*[13]

This doesn't mean we have to change our actions outwardly or move to the other side of the river so to speak, but it does require an inner shift: to see others as whole beings, not as ideologies or roles. We don't lose ourselves by expanding our perspective unless our identity is wrapped up in a particular belief system. If we identify too strongly with a viewpoint, it can feel threatening to acknowledge the goodness and integrity in someone on the "other side." But we are more than our beliefs and conditioning. Our true selves are not defined by them.

When my father was alive, he and I often saw the world differently. Since his passing, I have heard his voice inside me offering loving guidance. Once, I heard him say, "You've been walking around with my voice in your head for too long. Let it go. I couldn't see the whole picture when I had a body that got in the way. Focus on what really matters. Let go of the rest. It's your life, not anyone else's."

What stood out was his reminder about the human body getting in the way of seeing the whole picture. It's like being in the river valley, unable to see the full sky because of hills or mountains obstructing the view. Our view might be very different from what our neighbors across the river or anywhere else in the world can see. Our physical limitations, beliefs, and conditioning can obscure our broader perspective.

Instead of relating to others through ideas or labels, can we see them as whole human beings, just like us, floating down the same river of life, each experiencing emotions, delusions, pressures, and suffering in our own ways? Our struggles may look different, but beneath the surface, we share the same human experience: clouds passing through the sky of awareness, momentarily concealing the light of our true nature.

The invitation is to wish for all beings to be well, happy, and free from suffering, even those on the "other side." This doesn't mean condoning harm or ignoring injustice. It means beginning with our own hearts and clearing what blocks our capacity to love. Then we can meet others with presence and compassion, as they are, not as our judgments make them out to be.

WAITING TO CROSS

The great thing about living on the river is having a front-row view of whatever is happening on the river. Over the past seventeen years, the river has become the landscape of my life. I have grown attuned to its changes—both the slow, sweeping crescendos of unfolding sunrises and sunsets, and the staccato, blink-and-you'll-miss-it appearances of a bald eagle, a great blue heron, a swan, or a passing boat.

Many mornings, I wake to rose or golden light cast on my bedroom walls: a signal that sunrise is peaking in vibrancy, just for a moment. I leap out of bed, grab my camera and maybe my tripod, and bolt outside to capture the magic before it fades. I can go from bed to river's edge, camera in hand, in less than two minutes.

But there is one thing that often slows me down: road traffic. Our house sits on a busy road that runs between us and the river. Certain times of day are heavier than others, and I often find myself having to wait for a break in the flow of traffic before I can cross.

When I'm fixated on a fleeting, spectacular sight, my first reaction is often frustration. I feel it in my body as sensations of tension and pulling forward, as if my mind is already at the river while my body is stuck at the roadside. The thought comes quickly: *I'm going to miss it! Come on, come on, come on!*

I can't stop the traffic between me and the river, but I can choose how to relate to it. So, I aspire to meet it with mindfulness. First, I drop out of my head and into my feet, feeling their contact with the ground. That awareness rises through my body like a slow wave. I soften the tension and take a few deep, steady breaths.

If I'm still waiting, I'm no longer rushing. My state of mind has shifted. I have planted myself in the present moment. I can be with what is out of my control and let the cars pass. Sometimes, I begin offering lovingkindness, silently sending well wishes to the people driving by: *May you be well. May you be safe.* This simple practice brings me out of frustration and into connection.

Yes, sometimes the magical moment passes before I have crossed the road. But it doesn't really matter because something else has opened up. The narrow beam of goal-oriented focus has widened into a more spacious awareness of what is here now. Maybe the sunrise pulled me outside not so I could photograph it, but so I could be more present.

Mindful photography is about much more than just seeing. It is about how we relate to

❖ waiting for the magical moment

❖ what interferes with the perfect shot

❖ missing the perfect shot.

Instead of mentally resisting what stands between me and what I want, I have come to see these moments of waiting as invitations. What I had my sights set on does not have to define the moment. There is so much more to the moment than what I want from it. I can loosen my grip on thoughts of how it *should* be and open to how it really is.

If the image I set out to photograph doesn't materialize, what else is waiting to be noticed? What do we overlook when we are focused on a particular thing?

So, instead of complaining in my head or gripping the thought *I have to get this shot*, I shift into *I get to*. I get to pause. I get to feel my feet on the ground. I get to breathe and let go of tension. I get to experience the beauty of the sunrise, even if I don't capture it. And in those little breathers, sometimes new insight, inspiration, or a fresh way of seeing will emerge.

There is a kind of grace in being in harmony with what is, even when it diverges from what we had hoped for. Every moment of waiting becomes a sacred pause. A chance to practice presence. A chance to remember we are already part of something vast, fleeting, and alive that is far greater than any single image or idea we hold of it.

PART THREE

Rhythms
of the River

A YEAR OF SUNRISE PHOTOGRAPHY

From August 2022 to August 2023, I committed to photographing the Hudson River sunrises from the same spot every morning. At the beginning, I had no idea how important the project would become, how it would give structure and purpose to my days, or how much I would learn by simply showing up and paying attention.

The inspiration came during a visit to Marblehead, a historic coastal town in Massachusetts that I frequent. When I am by the ocean, I rarely miss a sunrise, no matter the season. In Marblehead, many locals are out early, walking, jogging, or pausing on the beach to take in the sunrise. I think of them as the "dawn patrol," fortunate to witness the sun rising over the Atlantic every day. For me, it always feels like a gift.

That trip made me wonder why I didn't do the same at home. Why wasn't I rising with the sun on the Hudson? Some mornings, I'd witness and photograph the sunrise but not with the eagerness that had me jumping out of bed on the coast. At home, I'd never made it an intentional practice. So, before leaving Marblehead, I resolved to begin a yearlong experiment. I would get up early every morning and photograph the river sunrise. The project began the first morning I was back home.

I set a few basic rules and made up more as time went on. For example, I would stand in the same spot: a small cement platform at the bottom of our riverside stairs. I would photograph both the blooming of the sunrise sky and the moment when sunlight first spilled over the horizon. And I would keep the composition consistent for as long as possible.

I had a rough sense of where the sun rises throughout the year: its northernmost point at the summer solstice and southernmost at the winter solstice. The widest lens I had for my camera couldn't capture the full range, but that was fine. The images were often more compelling and detailed when I used a wide, rather than an ultra-wide, lens.

Eventually, I would have to shift the frame as the sunrise moved north, over the trees across the river, near the summer solstice. But I'd figure that out when the time came. I also decided to always use a tripod, and to keep the aperture consistent.

Another rule: I wouldn't make pictures on fully overcast or foggy mornings when the sun wasn't visible. Not only were those photos visually dull, but thick fog made it impossible to focus, unless something like a boat or a group of geese floated through the foreground.

That said, I also had to know when to break the rules. Sometimes, the most breathtaking skies extended beyond the frame I had set. When the clouds, fog, or light took up more space, first I would photograph the standard composition. Then I would switch to the ultra-wide lens on my iPhone, generate a panorama, or take overlapping vertical shots with my DSLR to stitch together later.

As it turned out, the river had its own say in the project. Occasionally, the water level rose above the cement platform, making it inaccessible. On those mornings, I stood as close as possible to the usual spot. When snow or high water left too little room for a tripod, I made do without. Luckily, it was a mild winter, so those instances were rare.

With those guidelines, and a willingness to adjust, I embarked on the sunrise project. The river had so much to teach me. And I was ready to begin.

FROM PROJECT TO PRACTICE

Though originally conceived as a photography project, my yearlong river sunrise project quickly became so much more. It shaped and became an integral part of my morning meditation practice.

The quiet moments of welcoming the new day offered a natural opportunity to set an intention and reflect on what matters most. In formal mindfulness meditation, we have an *anchor*, such as the breath, the body, or sounds, to help steady our attention and return to when we notice the mind has wandered. It's like a home base. Bringing our meditation practice outdoors opens up more options for anchoring our attention.

We might also touch in with our deepest aspiration: how we want to live, how we want to express our energy in the world. There is potent energy in the morning air. Whatever had unfolded or failed to materialize the day before, each morning offered a fresh beginning, full of possibility. It became a time to inquire: *Where do I most need to shine the light of awareness and compassion? What needs attention now?*

One of my deep aspirations was to cultivate the insight of *interbeing*, the recognition that all things are interconnected and interdependent, by practicing the Five Mindfulness Trainings from the Plum Village tradition.[14] Zen master Thich Nhat Hanh described the Five Mindfulness Trainings as the most concrete ways to bring mindfulness into everyday life. Sitting on the riverside each morning became an invitation to reflect on or recite them, and to recommit to practicing them as best I could.

Meditation can be done with eyes closed or open. Waiting for the moment when the sun emerged over the bridge or trees was an opportunity to practice open-eye meditation: watching the sky canvas transform, the clouds drift, the water flow, the ice melt. Or I might close my eyes and turn my attention to the soundscape—the mix of natural and human-made sounds, including birdsong and traffic—allowing each sound to come and go. Other times, I practiced holding multiple sense doors in awareness: sight, sound, scent, the touch of air on my skin. There was always something to notice arising, transforming, dissolving from moment to moment. By the end of the project, I had cultivated a deeper awareness of *impermanence*: the wisdom that everything is in constant flux, and nothing stays the same.

We live on a busy road, and including the full soundscape in my awareness challenged me to allow all sounds to exist, not just the ones I found pleasant. This practice nurtured *equanimity*, a quality that allows us to meet each moment without reactivity or resistance and avoid generating unnecessary suffering. Equanimity also involves letting go of expectations, especially the impulse to judge whether a sunrise was a "good" one or not.

Each morning brought a range of possibilities, from muted to awe-inspiring skyscapes. I couldn't predict how the sunrise sky would unfold. Could I meet it just as it is, without comparison or commentary? And if I did slip into judging or thinking, how soon could I return to the raw sensory experiences of color, light, and sound?

If you were to drive past our section of the river, there is so much you would miss, for there is always more unfolding than meets the eye. But sitting still on the riverbank morning after morning attuned me to the subtlest changes: the rising and falling water level, the turning of leaves, the behavior of wildlife, the shifting ice. I began to sense the nuances of each season, each day.

I also basked in gratitude. Every morning offered something to appreciate: fog curling and rising over the water, the changing colors of the sky, birdsong, a frozen ripple etched in ice. In

winter, I often lingered longer than in any other season, captivated by the crystalline patterns along the shoreline.

The riverside photography project nourished my meditation
practice in countless ways. It helped me cultivate interbeing,
impermanence, equanimity, and gratitude. More than a photo
collection, this project became a devotional act: a daily return to
presence, intention, and awareness. As the seasons turned and
the light shifted, I wasn't just documenting the river reflecting
the sunrise sky. I was embodying the practice of waking up,
again and again, to what is.

THREE WAYS TO SEE A SUNRISE

W atching the sunrise bloom over the river is one of my favorite open-eye meditations. It offers a vivid illustration of three aspects of mindfulness practice:

❖ noticing what is arising and passing

❖ noticing how we are relating to what is arising and passing

❖ understanding the nature of what is arising and passing.

Still images are simply snapshots of fleeting moments. On any given morning when I am on the riverside with my camera, I might catch or miss the most stunning moment of the sunrise. So, the first level of practice is simply to notice what is happening, moment by moment. I note the movement of clouds, the changing light, the vehicles crossing the bridge. Within a single minute, there might be birds flying overhead, ripples in the water, a sudden breeze on my skin. Then there are the sounds: wind, birdsong, engines. And scents: damp earth, flowers, river air. There is so much to be aware of.

The second level of practice is to notice how I am relating to what is happening. Am I annoyed by the traffic noise? Wishing the traffic on the bridge would clear before the colors in the sky fade, so I can photograph a peak moment? Comparing this sunrise to yesterday's spectacular one? Hoping the clouds and light will align just right? Disappointed because it is a visually dull morning? Thinking it might be better elsewhere? Or simply caught up in what's next on my to-do list? How am I holding this moment?

The third level goes deeper: gaining insight into the nature of what is arising and passing. Understanding what thoughts are. Understanding the nature of clouds, light, and atmospheric conditions.

For example, during the Adirondack Balloon Festival, I became fascinated with how hot air balloons navigate. I listened to frequent festival updates to anticipate whether they would lift off each morning and evening. Balloons can't fly safely in the rain or above a certain wind speed. I learned that pilots rely on wind currents at different altitudes, adjusting their height to change direction. Balloons drift wherever the wind takes them, but skilled pilots use their knowledge to guide the journey with surprising precision.

At the same time, every balloon flight is an adventure. Meteorological conditions offer only a general sense of the flight path. Exactly where the balloon will land is not known in advance.

Learning about hot air balloons helped me better understand the movement of clouds, and why my sunrise predictions were often wrong. Many times, I assumed a gap in the clouds would remain, and it would allow the sunlight through within minutes. But it didn't because the gap closed. My understanding of how clouds move was flawed.

One balloon festival evening, I paddled upriver to meet Jack in a spot where the balloons might be visible. We decided not to drive around chasing them but to keep it simple and enjoy our river time instead. Whether we would see any balloons depended on the wind. My intention was to stay open and not fixate on a particular outcome. If I focused too hard on finding balloons, I might miss other photography opportunities, like the elusive great blue heron.

As it turned out, I did see a heron, who let me get unusually close. I became fixated on getting a shot of him taking off, and missed that moment because it happened too fast for me to lock in focus. I paddled away feeling . . . miffed. At the heron. Which, of course, was absurd.

It reminded me of watching the previous morning's glorious sunrise and thinking I could have been at the festival, photographing balloons lifting into that breathtaking sky. If I could have a do-over, I'd simply choose to be present with what was there.

Eventually, we spotted many balloons in the distance, floating over the river like a dream. I had never seen that before. It was a magical moment.

On the way home, we encountered the heron again, perched on a branch. He let us get just as close. Jack, who hadn't seen him earlier, was having a transcendent moment. But I was still annoyed about the missed photo and said aloud, "I'm not playing that game again, mister. I'm not even taking out my camera." It felt irreverent to speak to a heron like that, but my excuse was that I was tired.

And yet, that moment illustrated something important: There are so many ways to hold a moment. Jack was in awe. And I, the meditation teacher, was in resistance.

Mindfulness practice is not only about noticing what is happening. That is the first step. But we can also observe how we are holding the moment in our hearts and minds. Is there grasping? Resistance? Comparison? Regret?

Can we gain insight into the nature of our experience? We might see the thoughts or assumptions that precede a shift in mood. And then, rather than clenching around a moment, we can soften. Let go. Lighten up. Open to the wider context: the bigger picture, the play of form and formlessness.

Even when the heron flies, the moment passes, or the sky doesn't turn out as we had hoped, there is still something to be gained from observing it all. When we catch our patterns and hold things lightly, with curiosity and humor, we are less likely to carry the weight of dissatisfaction down the river with us.

Each moment is an invitation to practice: to notice, to relate, and to understand.

SLEEP AND YOU'LL MISS IT

Apparently, the sunrise that November morning was out-of-this-world spectacular. I say *apparently* because even though I had been remarkably disciplined about photographing the sunrise every day for the past three months, I missed that one.

I didn't photograph the river sunrise on fully overcast mornings or when I was away, obviously. But this was the first sunrise I missed that did not fall into either of those categories. The reason? I chose to sleep.

It was a busy time, and I had been burning the midnight oil. Still, I woke up every morning, without an alarm, just as the first colors began to appear in the sky. And every morning but that one, I rolled out of bed and made my way to the river with camera and tripod in hand. After photographing the peak moment, I'd crawl back into bed and sleep a little longer before starting the day.

That morning, I stirred at the usual time and checked the weather app, which predicted a cloudy sunrise. I peeked out the window and doubted the forecast for a second, but I was tired and went back to sleep.

Later, when I woke up for real, everyone seemed to be talking about the astonishing sunrise and how they had never seen *that* kind of orange before. Remember those "I could've had a V-8" commercials from the 1970s and '80s? That's exactly how it felt. I could've witnessed it . . . but I didn't.

There was no going back to capture that breathtaking sunrise. But I could learn from it.

Maybe it was the wake-up call I needed to start saying no to the late-night second winds that kept me up too long. This project mattered to me, and I hadn't shown up for it that morning. But the slip-up was clarifying. Instead of a photograph, I came away with a story and a fresh wave of motivation.

We can't rewind time and make different choices, but we *can* choose how we relate to the past. We can meet it with awareness, with self-compassion, and with the resolve to be more present next time.

So that's what I did. And for the rest of my yearlong sunrise photography project, I didn't sleep through another noteworthy sunrise.

FASCINATED BY ICE

L iving on the bank of the Hudson River is like having a front-row seat to a stage that is always in motion, constantly shifting. This is true even in winter, though you may have to slow down and get very close to notice.

For the entire year that I photographed the sunrise over the river every morning, I made a practice of noticing the subtle changes from one day to the next: *The river is like this right now.* It became part of my meditation practice. There were so many possibilities to focus on: sound, clouds, fog, wildlife, surface texture, reflection, water level.

Most winters, the river's surface freezes solid for a time. But during that year, it remained largely unfrozen, except for the delicate ice formations along the shoreline. I zoomed in, fascinated by their ever-changing details. Often, I lingered long enough to witness the sun's rays warming the ice, melting one frozen wave at a time back into liquid: a wonderful visual meditation.

The funny thing was, I often stayed longer on the coldest mornings because the ice patterns were so compelling. Many days, I returned to the river multiple times, bringing different lenses, to explore the fascinating textures and shapes. Focused on seeing and photographing the ice, the cold barely registered with me.

Each morning revealed something new: patterns that resembled delicate glasswork, frozen hourglasses, translucent bells. Some days, the ice was still. Other days, it moved, with larger plates shifting in the current, or fragile shards gliding like shattered glass.

One morning stood out above all the rest. As I photographed the intricate formations at the river's edge, a mass of delicate ice plates floated toward me. They slid over the ice already in place, creating a stunning, layered composition.

But it wasn't just how the ice looked; it was how it sounded. When the river carried what looked like "ice pancakes" or delicate plates downstream, they clicked together and sounded like a crackling fire—sometimes soft and rustling, other times roaring and percussive. These were the mornings when the river sang in its most glorious voice. The ice became floating chimes, playing winter's song.

Often, I stayed to meditate on the soundscape, letting my attention rest on the ice music. I made it a mindfulness practice to allow the less pleasant sounds like road noise and barking dogs to be there without disturbing my awareness, holding them as part of life's symphony. Sometimes, I focused on the sound of the ice or my own breath, the way you might tune in to a single instrument in an orchestra. Other times, I opened my attention wide, taking in the full soundscape with equanimity.

Even on overcast days when the sky didn't offer much for sunrise photography, I still ventured to the water's edge, wondering what new ice formations might be waiting. Photographing riverside ice not only carried the momentum of the sunrise project through the winter months, but it became a project in its own right. After the year ended, I exhibited my ice images, a testament to winter's often unnoticed artistry.

The ice taught me that there is always something to be amazed by on the river, even in the starkness of midwinter. After the floating ice chimes melt away, the songbirds return. Nesting eagles perch in the treetops overlooking the river as spring approaches. There is always something to savor.

Shared Joy

Anytime I stood by the river witnessing an amazing sunrise, I knew I was not alone in experiencing awe. I'd anticipate my social media feeds filling with images of the same sky, captured from different perspectives. It was inevitable. Knowing that the magical moment was being shared by many was one of the great joys of my sunrise photography project.

From my platform, I often looked east toward Washington County, imagining friends there witnessing the blooming sky from their own vantage points. I thought of others, too, in different directions and locations—people I just knew would be outside, cameras in hand, gazing upward. The collective delight felt almost tangible, like a current moving through the air.

The March 25th sunrise was the most stunning one of the year. I stood there steeped in astonishment as the reflective landscape shifted like a living kaleidoscope. I breathed in, not only the breathtaking sky, but the shared joy I imagined. It filled my body, heart, and mind, and felt like it was being absorbed into every cell of my being. And then I breathed out a simple, heartfelt wish: *May the breath of this sunrise reach all who need some grace today.*

How many mornings do we essentially blink and miss the magic, unaware that it even happened? How often do we fail to stand still long enough to let awe wash through us, rushing on because we believe there is something more important to do, somewhere else we are supposed to be? Or we become so focused on recording the moment for later that we are not fully present for it as it happens.

Sharing a magical moment, whether online or in conversation, extends the joy. It reminds others that these moments *do* happen. That even amid all the challenges and conflict, there is beauty in this world.

When you find yourself in a moment of wonder, be still. Drink it in fully. Pause between photos to simply *be here now.* These moments are gifts, freely given for our renewal.

What better reason to leave the house a little early, or build a little breathing room into your day, so you can stop if something wonderful appears?

And if you miss it, or if you are having a hard day, remember this: Somewhere in the world, someone is taking in the beauty of a sunrise or any other lovely thing and sending out a wish for the well-being of all beings. I like to think that those intentions collect into a band of energy, circling the world even now. So, if you need some of that energy, reach out. It's already here, waiting for you to help yourself to it.

SUMMER SOLSTICE SUNRISE

The summer solstice sunrise was one of the four most highly anticipated sunrises of my yearlong photography project. It marked the northernmost point of the sun's path in the sky. In all my years of living by the river, I had never photographed the solstice sunrise before; it happened so early. After that morning, the sun would begin its slow, southward journey once again.

For nearly a year, I had organized my life around photographing the sunrise, and this one felt especially significant. When I imagined creating a slideshow of a year's worth of river sunrises, the solstice seemed like a natural place to begin.

At the time, my daughter, Jasmine, was pregnant, due on July 5th. I had promised to be there for her during labor and birth, just as I had been when her first child—my first grandchild—was born.

A few days before the solstice, she was admitted to the hospital for an induction due to signs of preeclampsia. But the induction was not working.

The day before the solstice, I was called to the hospital. She and her partner, Nick, had already been there for forty-eight hours and were exhausted. If labor didn't begin soon, there was talk of sending her home.

Even after I arrived, things were not progressing. I found myself thinking about the solstice sunrise and wondering whether I would be there for it. I felt a pang of disappointment. At the same time, the idea of having a solstice-born grandson made me smile.

But the birth would happen when it happened. It was out of my control. And as meaningful as the solstice sunrise was, supporting Jasmine and being present for my grandson's birth mattered more.

That evening, I stepped outside for a short walk. While I was gone, the obstetrician broke Jasmine's water, and labor came on fast. When I returned, everything had changed. Contractions were in full swing. It looked like he would be born soon, perhaps before the solstice.

As it turned out, Kyler was born shortly after midnight—a summer solstice baby after all. But I need to offer a trigger warning. His birth was traumatic, the saddest thing I have ever witnessed. He survived, but he was born limp and unresponsive. It took seven long minutes for a neonatal resuscitation team to get him breathing on his own.

Because he had been without oxygen for so long, carbon dioxide had built up in his brain. He was transferred to Albany Medical Center to undergo seventy-two hours of cooling therapy, a treatment that reduces brain injury and improves long-term outcomes.

I left the hospital in the early morning hours, shaken. I wished there were someone to talk to, but the world was asleep, and I did not want to wake anyone up. Jasmine and Nick had each other. I felt so alone and worried. So, while driving home, I focused on my breath and a simple mantra to help me stay grounded: *This is how life is right now. It's part of being human.*

And I prayed.

At first, I didn't know what to pray for. What did I have a right to ask for on behalf of another? I don't know what any soul needs to experience in this life. I started with *Help!* And then it flowed from there.

May he be safe from inner and outer danger.
May he be protected.
May his care team be guided to make the best decisions.
May he be well.
May his brain and body be healthy.
May he be surrounded by love and light.
May his parents be surrounded by love and light.
May their suffering be eased.

It was out of my hands. All I could do was find the right prayer and take the widest view I could.

I arrived home just as the sky was beginning to lighten. At first, I went inside and lit a candle on my meditation altar overlooking the river. But I needed to be outdoors. The river was calling.

I carried the candle down to the riverbank and sat beside it, sending prayers downstream to the neonatal intensive care unit (NICU) where Kyler's tiny body was being cooled. I listened to the soothing sounds of the dawn chorus and watched the water flow as the solstice sky gradually brightened. The river held my pain and carried my prayers.

How remarkable that I could be present for both Kyler's birth and the solstice sunrise. That sunrise was among the earliest of the year, and I was there, photographing every stage of it. I watched the sky transform until the sun peeked over the trees across the river, tinting the landscape gold. The long-awaited moment had arrived.

Eventually, Jack woke up, and I was able to share the story and receive some emotional support. Then I tried to get some sleep. But I kept a candle lit by the river the entire time Kyler was in the NICU, and I continued to send prayers down the river for his healing, and for the care team tending to him.

When I think back to that morning, I wish I could have known what I know now: Things would be okay. The cooling therapy would go well. His brain scans would look good. But that is not how life works. We cannot see into the future.

What we can do in times of suffering is find strength and clarity in the present moment by turning toward something larger than ourselves: something vast enough to hold our raw, tender emotions. Even in the middle of the night, when the world is asleep.

That solstice morning, the river was my refuge. And I am forever grateful.

The summer solstice sunrise turned out to be the most significant sunrise of the year, not only for the light it revealed and its position in the landscape, but for what it helped me bear.

END OF THE PROJECT

My river sunrise photography project officially ended on August 6, 2023.

August was an odd month. I didn't feel like myself: a little off, a little down. Eventually, I realized that wrapping up the project was probably a big factor. For a whole year, it had added structure and meaning to my life. Without it, I felt a bit adrift.

After taking a few weeks off, I decided to continue the practice in a more relaxed way. Rule number one: Prioritize sleep. I hoped that understanding the value of the practice would motivate me to get to bed at a reasonable hour.

I liked the idea of photographing sunrises from wherever I happened to be, not just from my platform on the river. Or maybe noting the days I didn't take a photo and seeing how many years it would take to collect a sunrise image for every day of the year. But mostly, I welcomed the shift toward a more relaxed relationship with the practice. Filling in the gap days is a goal I am holding loosely.

Creating slideshows from the collection of images was deeply satisfying. They told a different, wider story than any single sunrise photo could. While each morning's sky held its own truths, the full collection revealed long arcs and shifting patterns painted with a broader brush. Movements and transitions that were invisible in a single frame came to life. The chronological series of images revealed how the sun's position on the horizon shifted, day by day: a subtle, graceful dance no single image expressed.

Reflecting on the year, I was struck by the value of giving something my daily attention. The project became a kind of refuge, something steady and sacred amid the changing tides of daily life. My mindfulness deepened, along with my sense of interbeing, discipline, and awareness of the ever-changing elements. Living beside the river became even more precious.

At the outset, I imagined winter would be the most difficult season to sustain the practice. However, that was not the case. While cold mornings required discipline at first, I often stayed longer, or even returned multiple times, because the ice formations were so captivating. I kept the stairs to the river clear, sometimes shoveling multiple times during a single storm.

Summer, on the other hand, proved to be the greatest challenge. The earliest sunrises happened around five o'clock. However, catching the most vibrant colors required waking up even earlier. I never would have imagined being fully awake and on the riverbank for the entire summer solstice sunrise, beginning when the first hint of light appeared in the sky. And yet, I was.

Because the sun rose so early, I often returned to bed afterward, sleeping later than intended, to ensure I got enough rest. Sometimes, that meant missing my usual outdoor exercise window when the temperatures were still bearable.

There were mornings I wasn't eager to get up and photograph the sunrise. But the greater pull of the project was strong enough to move me. That greater pull got me up and onto the riverside every morning there was a visible sunrise. It gave structure to my days. That kind of willpower lives in all of us. We just need to attach it to something meaningful enough to matter.

Perfectionism showed up from time to time in the form of high standards and judgments of "not good enough." For example, one morning I had just come out of a dream and forgot to check the camera settings, resulting in a slightly zoomed-in image that didn't match the rest of the collection. Such moments were invitations to practice letting go of perfectionism. They reminded me to ask what really mattered, and what was within my control. As the year went on, I grew more relaxed and more at peace with "good enough."

One worry that lingered throughout the project was the potential dismantling and reconstruction of the steel deck bridge that figures so prominently in my sunrise compositions. It didn't happen. But the concern generated by rumors became part of my mindfulness practice. Over time, I realized that worrying was neither necessary nor helpful. If or when the time came for bridge work, I trusted I would adapt and adjust accordingly. Trusting in the wisdom that emerges through presence became an antidote to worrying about things I couldn't change.

Here are a few takeaways from this journey of showing up every day for the rising sun:

❖ When something feels like a wholehearted *yes*, I will brave below-zero temperatures and snow-covered stairs to show up for it, day after day.

❖ The sunrise sky is a teacher of impermanence, offering lessons in both predictability and surprise.

❖ In general, the most stunning sunrises require just the right amount of clouds.

❖ During a long stretch of overcast winter mornings, I couldn't photograph the sunrise at all. The days felt bleak. But eventually, the clouds parted, and I appreciated the sun's return even more. This made me reflect on the metaphorical role of clouds in our lives.

❖ When the sky turns fuchsia or brilliant orange, there isn't time to run inside to get a different camera for a panoramic shot before the colors fade. Don't even try. Better to stay put and be present.

Most of all, experiencing the sunrise reminded me daily of who I am and how to shine.

In the end, it wasn't just a year of collecting sunrises; it was a year of deepening presence. A year of meeting each morning as it was, just as I was. A year of being aware of the sky, the river, and my own rhythms. Though the formal project came to an end, its essence continues. It's the invitation to keep showing up for the blossoming of a new day—with or without a camera.

Lost and Found

About a year after the photography project ended, I remembered something I had forgotten: how nourishing it is to wake up early and experience the sunrise on the river.

During the project, I wouldn't have imagined writing that sentence. When the project ended, I relished the freedom of sleeping in. But I also felt an emptiness where that daily ritual had been.

Since then, I have created slideshows from the images, given presentations, and even exhibited my winter river ice photography: a sub-project that emerged from my early morning practice. And yet, since the project ended a year ago, I have only photographed twenty-two Hudson River sunrises.

Yesterday morning, for the first time in more than four months, I photographed one again. It wasn't planned. I didn't set an alarm. I just woke naturally at 5:30 to a sky canvas that demanded my attention. I hesitated. *Do I really want to grab my camera and tripod?* This time, the answer was *yes*.

So, I walked down to the river, took a few pictures, and lingered. I felt the cool morning air on my skin and listened to the dawn chorus. Birdsong and insect symphonies merged under a sky brushed with rose and lavender.

Oh, how I had missed this.

I had planned to go back to sleep afterward but instead stayed to watch the first rays of sunlight. Then I went for an early morning paddle. It felt incredible. Naturally, I wondered: *Why haven't I been doing this all summer?* What happened? How did I slip into the habit of kayaking later in the day when the sun was hotter and the experience less enjoyable?

What happened? It is an important question that requires care. There is a big difference between self-inquiry and self-judgment.

With mindfulness, we notice when our mind has wandered, usually into the past, future, or a narrative about the present. Then we return to the here and now, where our power is. But sometimes, looking into the past can be useful if we do it to gather information and see clearly, so we can live more aligned with our deepest aspirations.

Make no mistake: Looking deeply is not ruminating. Regret, blame, and self-loathing can sneak in through the back door, pulling us into a loop that does not serve us. Looking deeply with mindfulness can help us to see clearly without getting stuck in unhelpful places, or to free ourselves sooner. It requires self-honesty.

We can investigate like a scientist gathering data, observing without judgment. If we find something undesirable, mindfulness offers tools to meet it with wisdom, compassion, and equanimity. We can welcome our discoveries as part of the human experience.

Looking deeply is like inspecting the inside of my kayak before setting out. I don't *want* to find uninvited passengers like snakes, mice, or spiders in there, but it is better to know so I can deal with them before I am on the water, when a startle response could tip me into the river. Similarly, when we reflect on our lives, we want to see clearly, without avoidance, but also without drowning in self-criticism. A trusted friend can sometimes help us see what we are missing. However, the key is choosing someone who cares about our well-being and is perceptive and honest, not someone who is characteristically critical, prone to soapbox speeches, or likely to say only what they think we want to hear.

When we look deeply in the right way, we can acknowledge that *here I am again, being human in this particular way*—for we all

have our patterns. Here I am being human . . . *and can I do better?*
Then make "doing better" an exciting, expansive invitation rather
than a reason to be unkind to ourselves or to make unfounded
generalizations about how uniquely flawed we are.

So, what *did* happen that led me to abandon the early morning river time that had been so enriching? It was a mix of staying
up too late and jumping straight into my to-do list instead of
prioritizing self-care. I let myself get drawn into other people's
business rather than tending to my own. In short, I lacked strong
enough outer *and inner* boundaries: old patterns that sometimes
creep back in when I am not adequately rested and resourced.
Like a persistent weed, they need regular tending, so they don't
get out of hand.

But in the cool, invigorating air that morning on the river, I
felt the contrast: the energy I had been missing. There is something potent about that time of day, something that makes me
feel alive, tapped in, receptive. Inspiration comes naturally. Ideas
flow.

For weeks, I had felt stuck, low on energy and creativity. And
the missing piece had been literally right in front of me the
whole time. How could I forget something so vital as my sunrise
practices?

Yet, there is value in forgetting. Rediscovering a supportive
practice allows us to feel, with clarity, the difference it makes.
And that contrast can inspire a deeper commitment, not from
guilt but from recognition of its worth.

It's just like meditation. When we realize our mind has wandered into a forest of thought, it is an invitation to meet ourselves with kindness rather than judgment. We can simply
acknowledge the moment of awareness and bring the mind back
to the here and now. It does not matter how many times the
mind has strayed; what matters is the returning.

A year after my river sunrise project ended, I now see what I have been missing:

❖ a daily meditation that sets the tone for my day

❖ an opportunity to engage with the potent morning energy

❖ an ideal time to kayak

❖ time to simply be—immersed in the natural world, beginning the day steeped in gratitude.

In other words, it has become clear that if I am not waking up early and experiencing the sunrise on the river regularly, I am forgoing what helps me to be at my best. To paraphrase the fourteenth-century Persian poet Hafiz: If you haven't been taking your medicine by doing your daily practices, how can anyone take your heartaches seriously?[15]

The daily work is in committing and recommitting to what nourishes us. Every time we honor something of value through our actions, we build trust in ourselves. And that, too, is a gift of my river sunrise project.

PREDICTABLY, SPRING

Once again, it was spring equinox. The first thing I saw when I sat up in bed and looked out the window was a pair of geese gliding silently upriver.

I stepped outside to photograph the sunrise from my usual spot. Yesterday, the cement platform I stand on was underwater. This morning, the water was a hairline below the top of it. Every year, the spring thaw swells the river: a predictable rhythm of the season.

As I stood there, the sun rose precisely in its equinox position. Once again, I spent the winter tracking the sunrise as it journeyed slowly northward, crossing the bridge from its southernmost point on the winter solstice. It happens every year, and I know exactly how far it will travel before reaching its northernmost position on the summer solstice.

The position of the sunrise on any given day is reliable. It's the cloud cover that changes from day to day, moment to moment. The clouds come and go, but the celestial movements remain steady.

Even after years of photographing river sunrises, I cannot predict which sunrises will be glorious. Different currents of clouds move at different altitudes, in varying directions. How they come together is all a matter of timing.

Any moment, we can choose to identify with the clouds that come and go or something more abiding, like the arc the sun travels through the sky or even the vast sky that holds it all. Even as the human world and its dramas feel wobbly, like a toy top losing momentum and tilting off-center, the natural world remains a steadying refuge. I remember those early weeks of

COVID when birdsong and the chorus of spring peepers across the river offered the most beautiful music to my ears, soothing reminders of continuity. Listening to them was a deep, nearly effortless meditation.

Amid the twists and turns of the human saga, there is this, too: the songbirds, the equinox sunrise, the spring peepers. If I were at the ocean today, I would see the waves still crashing against the shore, the tide still ebbing and flowing. These stable patterns of the natural world offer themselves as a refuge, a lesson in resilience, a reminder to return to what is steady and true. By grounding ourselves in these steady rhythms, we can meet the ever-changing human world with greater stability and freshness.

Spring Equinox

Summer Solstice

Fall Equinox

Winter Solstice

ON THE RIVER IN THE MORNING

When I am on the river in the morning
paddling through calm water,
the wordless perfection of birdsong
reminds me: There is no need
for verbal elegance here.
Just sing.

A few deeply felt, simple words
are enough. Their truth
is not diminished if lost
on anyone or everyone else.
Perhaps you must be here
to truly understand.

Here, there is no need
for sophistication or striving,
no need to impress.
Conflict makes no sense.
Here is untangling,
uncomplicating,
being real.
Being gratitude.
Being presence.
Being love.

What will light up the heart today?
The river's reflection
dancing across sunlit leaves?
The stillness of a heron?
Or something entirely new:
some new reflection
the natural world offers
to reveal a truth, to help
make more sense of this life.

IN THE MORNING FOG

All around my kayak,
fog rises into clouds
that will release their tears
into the flowing river.

River, tell me
what I need to know.
What letting go,
what new understanding
rises this morning
with the fog?
What seeks illumination?

Love, fill me with courage
to stop giving away my power,
to say no to the merely familiar
that stands in the way
of this unambiguous yes.

Busy mind, *shhh*.
It is time to surrender.

Body, keep paddling
until all that exists
is the sound of paddle blade
moving through water,
and the wild, winged
symphony all around.

Then—be still.
Listen some more.

Floating Under the Moonless Sky

Oh, the bliss of being out on the river during late sunset. It is getting dark, and the colors in the sky are vivid. I float in my kayak, surrounded by birds singing their goodnight songs and frogs croaking from the wetland across the river. A sweet, unidentified floral fragrance lingers in the air. Two beavers have swum by. I feel peaceful, weightless. My breath slows and deepens.

In this moment, I have not a care in the world. Everything feels just right. Hushed. My personal concerns seem far away, unable to reach me out here. I smile, filled with delight, as the colors deepen from moment to moment. Being under this sky is like watching an enormous Polaroid picture developing.

Today was long: an eleven-hour workday. The school year is ending, and there is so much to attend to in the coming days that my head spins just thinking about it. But right now, I am not thinking. Just being.

The first light to appear is from an airplane. Its reflection glides across the water like the flight of a mosquito, bounced around by gentle ripples.

Just a month ago, I marked the first anniversary of my mother's passing. Grief reached a depth I had not known before, settling heavy in my bones. And now, to my amazement, I feel an equivalent sense of lightness and joy. That is the nature of grief, and the value of simple pleasures that impart a buoyancy to our life.

A line from Kahlil Gibran's *The Prophet* floats through my mind:

The deeper that sorrow carves into your being, the more joy you can contain.[16]

What I feel now is not a buzzing happiness but a full-bodied joy steeped in tranquility. When you have been as low as I have been recently, you appreciate this kind of upliftment. It feels like a blessing.

The birdsong softens, a long decrescendo as evening settles in. Fewer birds sing now. I notice two bright pinpoints in the sky. At first, I think they are planes, but after a few minutes, I realize they are celestial bodies: maybe Venus and Jupiter. One is larger and brighter, the other smaller and fainter, hanging higher in the sky.

Out here, it is hard to tell what is moving and what is stationary. I am drifting. The clouds are shifting. The lights above appear to move, too, but perhaps it is just everything else moving around them.

As the sky darkens and the air cools, I am struck by the wildness of being alone on this great river beneath the darkening sky, surrounded by sound and stillness. I feel so alive, tingling with vitality. Surely this spacious serenity is my more natural, open state—the real me. It feels like being Home.

Star light, star bright,
First star I see tonight,
I wish I may, I wish I might,
Have this wish I wish tonight.

I pause to inquire: What does my heart wish for? *To follow love, not fear.* To feel, right now, what it is like to let that energy flow freely, like this river. Imagining this makes my whole body smile, radiant with aliveness.

Toward the swamp, where frogs croak in the distance, I catch a flicker of light. At first glance, I mistake it for car head-lights on the road. But no—it's the glow of fireflies! They have begun their nightly ritual, flashing their light in the darkness, searching for connection.

The light show begins. Birds have gone quiet. The sky is nearly black. There will be no moonlight tonight.

A few stars twinkle overhead. Fireflies flash below. All these tiny points of light are reflected, as if by a huge mirror, on the river's surface. Some fireflies stay near the ground, while others hover at the treetops. I am drawn to the rippling light on the water, the reflection of the last remaining light in the sky. Light and darkness dance together in a silent, undulating rhythm.

Ahead, I detect the barely visible form of a beaver gliding through shadows. Only the interplay of light and water reveals its presence. If I were to paddle now, it might slap its tail: a loud, percussive note joining the swamp's nighttime symphony.

The last trace of light fades, and I paddle gently back toward the dock. This is such a different state of consciousness from the gravity of being on land.

The sense of inner homecoming stays with me as I make my way back to my yard: a feeling of already being home before I've even arrived. In the backyard, hundreds of fireflies flicker and blink in a spectacular light show—an extension of the river's bliss. It looks magical, like a field of fairy lights. I stand in wonder, delight washing through me.

It's the perfect welcome, reminding me that peace is not something I have to leave behind on the river. It lives within me, ready to return to whenever I pause, breathe, and allow myself to simply be.

Moonlit Symphony

Now the full moon
and not having anywhere to
be in the morning
lure me to the dock, where
waves lap softly against
the shore: liquid middle voice.
Invisible breeze passes
through foliage turning trees
into soft rustling tambourine bass
as buzz of night-singing insects
become egg shakers gliding
along the top this gently
percussive evening.

The round moon swims slowly,
steadily through a sea
of illuminated clouds
until it rests, floating
in an ocean of dark blue,
luminous and full.

Reflections of moonlight
on the wavy surface below
shimmer like fireflies along with
thousands perhaps millions of real
fireflies flickering in the yard,
becoming stars in the sky:
so many kinds of light!

Glowing moon moves
perceptibly between the first
two of five parallel power lines.
Since I sat down, it has floated
twenty degrees along
its celestial arc, touches
the first line like a note
on a musical staff
and continues up the scale.

Listen, says the night,
to the moonlit symphony.
Come out and sit for a while
in deep blue, luminous
splendor, where all is
thank you
thank you
thank you.

BEADS OF DEW

River fog rises
this chilly morning
through silky webs,
clinging as beads of dew
on fine, spiral chains:
each a droplet once more,
revealing woven designs.

Oh, the joy of being
a single drop
when the light shines through—
glistening, gleaming!
Then shrinking, evaporating,
lifted by heat and light
back to vapor—
lighter, rising!

Rising, falling,
river, fog, cloud,
droplet.

Friend, tell me:
Do you remember
when we were a river
flowing toward the ocean?

IN THE MORNING MIST

Early autumn mornings tend to be dramatic on the river, often featuring mist. The calm water becomes a dark, sprawling stage where steam fog performs a spirited ballet. From my dock, I have a front row seat. It reminds me of the many New York City Ballet performances I have seen at the Saratoga Performing Arts Center throughout my life. The mist moves with the same grace and unity. The soundtrack features the sprawling, seasonal ritardando of the last few crickets and a variety of birdsong solos.

It often seems that individual mist dancers break away from the mass, twirling alone or spinning in small circles with others, yet all belonging to one choreography and rhythm: one dance with many parts. A misty figure may break away in a vigorous pirouette, like a tiny whirlwind, before rejoining the rest of the ensemble. When sunbeams slip through the trees, they cast spotlights onto the dancers, illuminating their circling movements.

Eventually, I can't resist. I slip into my kayak and glide across the dark, reflective stage, adorned with clusters of lily pads and ribbons of aquatic grasses. The dancers lift and twirl all around me. It is sheer delight, especially when I paddle toward the sun, with the mist swirling in the foreground.

One morning, already enraptured by the mist dancing all around me, I passed beneath the bridge and spotted a great blue heron standing like a statue amid the whirling movement: a striking counterpoint of stillness. Fortunately, I had the foresight to bring my camera that day.

Misty autumn mornings on the river are a gift. To engage with the cool air, the glowing sunrise, the still water, and the dancing mist is to begin the day in deep harmony with both outer and inner nature.

Autumn Releasing Ritual

In autumn, when the foliage reaches its peak, any day might be the last day of kayaking season, making each outing feel even more precious. One late October day, I paddled my usual route along the river, searching for leaves illuminated just right by the low, late afternoon sun. The maples and other deciduous trees already had passed their prime. Now it was the oaks' time to shine.

I was drawn to a particular spot beneath an oak tree, where I could step out of my kayak and stand on a small patch of shore. I lingered there, absorbing the rich red hues of the oak leaves and the gentle movement of the water. A light breeze sent many leaves twirling and gliding downward, where they settled on the shore or floated away with the current.

With deep appreciation, I savored the warmth of the sun on my skin and the sweet, rhythmic music of the lapping waves. Then an idea came to me.

Surrounded by fallen oak leaves, I felt inspired to do an impromptu releasing ritual. I gathered a handful of leaves and, one by one, offered them to the wind and water. With each leaf, I spoke aloud something I was ready to release or already had let go of: old fears, outdated stories, lingering habits, even certain kinds of conversations.

I didn't release the next leaf until the previous one felt complete. Some I watched float away until they were out of sight. As they drifted, I felt them lose their hold on me, and a greater sense of inner freedom and joy arose. With distance and time, the river of life really does pull things away from us, helping us soften our attachments, move on, and make space for something new.

It had been a month of profound letting go. Longstanding anxieties, cravings, and patterns that no longer served were falling away, just like the autumn leaves. For example, after years of avoiding doctors, I'd recently mustered up the courage to keep my appointments—and that morning had an anxiety-provoking medical test. Despite feeling nervous, I showed up. That afternoon, as I stood beneath the oak tree, something shifted. A stronger, freer energy was palpable.

I celebrated these changes, honoring my decision to break habits that had kept me stuck, to follow my inner guidance rather than fear, to set inner and outer boundaries where they were needed. Alongside the trees, I was letting go, in perfect timing. It felt incredible.

Feeling lighter, I paddled home, singing a mantra: *I release what no longer serves me.*

When I arrived home, I checked my email and received news that felt like a direct affirmation of my transformation: I had been selected for a photography exhibition at a gallery I'd long dreamed of showing my work in. The timing felt almost magical, too perfect to be a coincidence.

Releasing what had held me back had created space for something new to arrive. The ritual had been more than symbolic; it was a turning point, a moment of stepping into my power. And just like that, life responded.

THE EXQUISITE ANGLE

It was one of those rare and ethereal frosty mornings on the river. I leapt out of bed, grabbed my camera, and was out the door in minutes. By the time I returned home, there was barely time to wash my face, let alone shower, before heading to work.

I would have loved to linger longer outdoors, but being on a schedule makes me more discerning about how to use my time. A narrow window of opportunity forces clarity: I do what matters most. And that morning, the most important hour of my day was spent driving along the river, chasing the light.

Sunlight, frost, and steam fog combined to create dazzling images—but only from certain angles. I searched for the precise perspective that illuminated the frosty trees in the most breathtaking way. Sometimes I spotted it from a distance, only for the magic to disappear when I got closer. A shift of position, and the frosty grandeur faded. Both in photography and in life, sometimes we need to step back to find the most inspired view.

One riverside property seemed to have the best view of all. I longed to drive up the private driveway, imagining the perspective from their yard. "They've got the whole view!" I grumbled.

Then I laughed at myself. The moment reminded me of an old church song, and I started making up verses:

They've got the frosty winter trees / in their yard,
They've got the frosty winter trees / in their yard,
They've got the frosty winter trees / in their yard,
They've got the whole view in their yard.

They've got the fog from the river / in their yard,
They've got the fog from the river / in their yard,
They've got the fog from the river / in their yard,
They've got the whole view in their yard.

My heart swelled with song and joy. And then I wondered: Were the people inside that house appreciating the view? Were they even aware of it? Was their perspective truly better than mine? Maybe not. Maybe the best view was right where I was. I kept driving and singing, stopping whenever I found just the right angle: the angle of *yes!*

Some of the most striking scenes were visible from the green steel deck bridge. With no shoulder or walkway, taking time to change lenses on the bridge wasn't an option. I had to be ready before stepping onto it, with lens chosen, aperture set, and vision clear. There wasn't time to play around creatively in such a narrow space, with nearly constant, two-way traffic.

The lens of awareness extends far beyond the camera. The deeper question is: How do I position myself, my heart, my awareness, to reveal beauty and inspiration? How do I find the angle that turns the present moment into a precious opportunity to awaken and express love?

On frosty mornings like this, I seek images that remind me of how life appears when seen from just the right perspective: when the light shines through and the scene becomes heaven on earth. Loving awareness transforms everything. It softens the edges, dissolves resistance, and invites freedom, even from my own beliefs about how things "should" be.

At one point during my drive, I turned on the radio just in time to catch song lyrics that were the most perfect words for that moment. I turned off the radio. *Message received.*

In this broader sense, finding the right angle means letting everything serve our awakening. It means shifting perspective: letting grudges and resentment soften into equanimity, even appreciation. It means replacing self-judgment with self-compassion, and frustration with others with the recognition that they, too, are fellow travelers on this messy human journey, worthy of both compassion and healthy boundaries. It means loosening resistance and trusting that every situation, no matter how painful, is offering something essential for our growth.

These are the little epiphanies that set things right in the heart. *Grace.* For me, it's all about awakening and evolving in love. Cultivating the wisest, most compassionate response possible to myself, to others, to whatever life brings. Holding my relationship to thoughts, emotions, and experiences differently, until they, too, are bathed in the light of love.

Reframing is key. Instead of regretful thoughts like "If only I hadn't . . . ," reach for gratitude:

> *I'm grateful for whatever it took to wake me up.*
> *I'm grateful this experience helped me discover my worth.*
> *I'm grateful it deepened my compassion and understanding.*
> *I'm grateful for the opportunity to awaken.*

Even difficulties can be transformed, with a simple mantra: *This, too, serves my awakening.* And then, all at once, the sunbeams kiss the frosted trees, the steam fog rises around it all, and awe, hope, and love flood in.

Boom! I've found the exquisite angle. The angle that sets me free and fills my heart with song. The angle that allows me to embrace life, exactly as it is, and to apply my heart and mind in ways that open up new possibilities.

That frosty morning drive was the most important hour of my day. But it wasn't just about the pictures. It never is.

THIS, TOO, SHALL PASS

There are many moments in my kayak, with my camera stowed in a waterproof bag, when something draws my attention. It might be trees illuminated just right. I consider taking out my camera but, for whatever reason, decide to catch it on the way back.

That almost never works out. Something about the river always changes—or as I once heard meditation teacher Joseph Goldstein say, "Everything is becoming otherwise." It truly never is the same river twice. I have learned to stop when something captures my eye, or to be at peace with missing out.

When you use any kind of recording device, or simply pay close attention, you become acutely aware of how quickly things change. Sensory impressions are constantly ebbing and flowing. The light shifts. Your vantage point changes. A breeze ripples the water's surface. Something subtle alters the mood or appearance of a scene.

There have been times I wanted to paddle through river fog or capture it in a photo. However, I decided to do something else first, and the moment passed. The fog lifted.

The river is a masterclass in impermanence, revealing it moment by moment. For instance, right now there is a breeze, and the water's surface is not as calm and reflective as it was just minutes ago.

The river teaches me to be present and act in the moment. Don't wait; conditions can change in an instant, and the scene may lose its splendor. Other times, by waiting a little longer, they may shift in surprising and lovely ways. *This, too, shall pass* is one of the river's many refrains that can be heard by ears that listen closely.

Once, a large, fallen tree got caught on the dam. It stayed there for nearly two years, wedged in place, until one spring as the river thawed, it was suddenly gone. The flowing ice must have carried it away. I wondered how long it would take to be freed. And then, it was.

Another time, I went out kayaking with the morning fog dancing all around me. The clouds and light came together perfectly. It was the kind of scene I live for . . . but my camera was at home. I promised myself I'd get back out at the same time the next day or when conditions were similar. That was nearly three years ago, and I am still waiting.

Conditions are never exactly the same. Subtle differences matter. If you see something you want to photograph, don't wait —because it will change. And if you tend to run late, what better reason to give yourself extra time? Leave a little room to pause.

Regardless of whether you have a camera, if you find yourself in a magical moment illuminated just right, pause to savor it. Taking in the good helps rewire the brain for positive *neuroplasticity*, a term that describes the brain's ability to adapt and change, even physically by creating new neural pathways and undergoing other structural changes.

I have photographed several hundred river sunrises, and no two have ever been alike. The river moves through cycles and patterns, but even on the same date, year after year, *something* is always different: the color of the light, the shape of clouds or ice, a branch that has fallen.

One March morning, I was immersed in photographing the partly iced river. I was captivated by a large sheet of ice around which smaller pieces flowed, sometimes touching and making a mesmerizing sound like smooth stones tumbling in ocean surf. Then the furnace repairman arrived, and I went inside.

When I returned a half-hour later, the great shelf of ice was gone. In its place was a flotilla of small ice plates flowing down-river in shimmering formation, as far as I could see.

The large ice mass had looked immovable. And yet, it vanished. I wondered how. Maybe chunks of ice collided with it. Maybe it simply broke apart. Maybe whatever happened was also responsible for freeing the tree at the dam.

You never know what will come floating down the river. And you never know what might enter your life to shift your perspective or dislodge what feels stuck. *This, too, shall pass* isn't just the river's song. It's also ours.

At times, our minds can convince us that things are hopeless, that we are headed in the wrong direction. But just like the ice and stuck tree, our thoughts can shift. A new insight can come along and empower us. Something unexpected can move us.

Several years ago, a situation in my life felt hopeless and impossible to transcend. But now it is just a memory. I see the situation, and the other party, in an entirely different light. The growth since then still feels remarkable, as does the shift in how I relate to it now.

March is a month that embodies impermanence. In like a lion, out like a lamb. Winter ends, and spring begins. The world wakes up again. The daffodils shoot up. The birds return. The river flows again.

This winter, the river remained frozen longer than in recent years. At times, it looked more like a snowy field than a flowing body of water. I missed seeing it flow. So, I turned my attention elsewhere. I began writing this book and going to yoga classes. Before I knew it, the ice melted. The river sparkled again.

But during the weeks I couldn't see it, the river was in the process of teaching me another lesson of impermanence. Everything is in flux, and timing is everything. Even when you think nothing is happening, the river, and you, are quietly becoming otherwise.

PART FOUR

The Inner River

MINDFUL PADDLING

Mindfulness is a portable practice. Bringing it to the river opens up a whole new dimension of presence.

Being outdoors, surrounded by the freshness and movement of the living world, makes it easier to stay rooted in the here and now. When our senses are engaged, presence arises more naturally. The touch of air on skin, the scampering and fluttering of wildlife, and the sounds of birdsong and wind through the trees, for example, all help to anchor awareness. Being outside also expands our frame of reference. Awareness extends beyond the body and the walls that enclose us and flows outward into the wider landscape.

I was paddling on the Hudson one gorgeous summer day when it occurred to me: If someone were to notice me out here, they would probably see me as part of the river's tranquility. Just a calm person having a calm moment in a peaceful place. What they wouldn't see were all the thought bubbles trailing behind me like in a cartoon. Did I say something I shouldn't have to a friend? What will I make for dinner? What needs to happen so I can be on time for my next commitment?

In contrast to the serenity surrounding me, my inner world was full of commotion. The irony wasn't lost on me. In guided meditations set in a peaceful place in nature, I usually imagine myself floating in my kayak on this very river. Yet there I was, actually on the river . . . but mentally somewhere else entirely. My mind was time-traveling to the past and future, caught in worries, hypothetical scenarios, and to-do lists.

It was a perfect opportunity to practice. I began noticing when and where my mind had wandered. Then I gently brought my attention back to the river itself, over and over.

Most often, I noticed my mind darting ahead into the future, into a tangle of "what ifs." Worry is, all too commonly, a deeply conditioned habit. It's fueled by what neuropsychologists call the brain's "negativity bias," which keeps us scanning for potential problems, dangers, and threats. It's what human minds do, and it's an ancient response. The good news is: With mindfulness, we can see it happening. *Hello, worry. Hello, habit energy. I see you.* We can pause, observe, and choose to come back to the present moment.

Each time I noticed the wandering, I brought my attention back home to this paddle stroke. To the sound of the paddle slicing through the water and the splash as it lifted. To the sensations in my shoulders, arms, and core. Can I be present for just this one stroke? And now this one?

Sometimes I imagined my paddle pushing thoughts downriver, away from me. Sometimes I played games with awareness: Can I paddle mindfully to that tree up ahead? How far can I paddle in presence before a thought snags me? It became a playful and curious experiment.

To steady awareness, I sometimes synchronized my breath with my paddling: inhaling for three strokes and exhaling for five. Or inhaling for four, retaining for four, exhaling for four, and pausing for four.

Mindfulness doesn't mean the mind won't wander. It means we notice when it does and gently return. We learn to recognize familiar loops and mental grooves. We witness the workings of our minds, so we're not carried down the stream of thought. Instead of getting lost in future scenarios, past moments, or stories about how things are, we begin again, right here, right now. Again and again.

This breath.
This stroke.
One moment of presence at a time.

RIVER REFUGE

Long ago, I came up with a term that describes the consciousness I experience on the river: *river bliss*. It refers to a
sense of buoyancy, peace, and interconnection with the world
around me that includes feeling the gentle rocking of the water
beneath my kayak and the solid stability that keeps me afloat.

At any time, there are countless forces in the world and
within myself that can weigh me down. Some days, gravity feels
stronger, and the water deeper, than other days. In challenging
and uncertain times, it becomes essential to have a refuge larger
than the waves of our personal and collective lives.

The river is my refuge. On difficult days, it helps restore balance and serenity. It has carried me through innumerable challenges and chapters of life. Situations that once seemed enormous
have drifted away like leaves floating downstream. Relationships,
jobs, and crises have come and gone. Since moving to the river,
so much water has flowed under the bridge, both literally and
metaphorically.

Not long ago, I faced a situation that felt overwhelming and
unsolvable. A friend reminded me, "A year from now, you won't
even remember all of this." She was right. It's the way of the
river. Sometimes we simply have to trust the flow.

One very intense day, forgotten until I came across an old
journal entry, ended with me on the river. The evening sky was
beautiful. A first-quarter moon floated in and out of clouds.
Thousands of fireflies sparkled along the riverside, and the
intoxicating fragrance of milkweed blossoms filled the air.

After resisting reality earlier that day, I spent the evening
practicing the opposite: literally going with the flow and letting

the river carry me. Surrendering to the current can be a marvelous practice for difficult days.

Sometimes I alternate between paddling and drifting, to feel the difference in both mindset and body. Part of the art of living is discerning when to exert effort and when to go with the flow.

If something feels particularly "sticky," it is wonderfully therapeutic to get in my kayak and paddle through it, breathing deeply. During my time as a kindergarten teacher, I called it *paddling for peace*. Exhaling troubling thoughts into the water and physically releasing the day's stress was essential self-care.

Several years ago, my mom was diagnosed with the illness that would take her life a few months later. It was winter, a time I couldn't go kayaking. Still, the sight of vibrant sunrises and frosted trees lining the river uplifted me through those sad and challenging days. When she was fading fast in the spring, river time fell by the wayside so I could be with her. After she passed, the river was there to embrace me.

In times of grief, I have found the ocean immense enough to hold whatever sorrows I bring to it. But when I can't be by the ocean, I offer my emotions to the river, pushing them along with my paddle and letting the current carry them to the sea.

When my beloved great-uncle Ralph passed away, I honored him with a sunset paddle. Though he lived more than 3,000 miles away in British Columbia, we shared a deep love of kayaking. Six years earlier, I had kayaked with him and my dear great-aunt June on the Sechelt Inlet, not knowing it would be his final time in a kayak after fifty-eight years of avid paddling. As I glided beneath a breathtaking sunset sky, I remembered him with gratitude and love. Our lives felt forever joined by the waterways of the world.

The river also held me in the early morning hours after my grandson's traumatic birth. It helped me to absorb difficult news more than once. The spaciousness of the water offered room to meet my reactions with presence and remember that I could return to the stillness and love within, beneath the surface of daily life.

One particularly charged morning comes to mind. I waited until I felt resourced and grounded on the river before checking the news. Kayaking alone, I didn't feel alone. A heron flew across the water. A bluejay chattered in the trees. A duck swam by, flapping its wings the whole time. A bald eagle soared over-head. A belted kingfisher perched on a fallen tree.

I was surrounded by beings simply living their lives, untouched by human drama. Yet I also felt connected to the long human history that has unfolded on and around this river. The wars, conflicts, innovations, and shifts in leadership were once big news for those who called the riverbanks home.

Spending time on the river when the world feels heavy is often exactly what my spirit needs. It places the news into a much wider frame. This, too, is part of the ever-changing current of history. It will come and go in its own time.

I feel blessed to have the river as a refuge. Over the years, I have offered it my grief, fear, frustration, sadness, and anger. All of it flows downstream toward the sea.

The river lifts me above the gravity of the world, allowing me to float. It reminds me that I, too, am mostly water—made to move, made to flow around obstacles. Water always finds a way.

When I am in my kayak, I feel the weight lift. My mind clears. My heart softens and expands. Spaciousness opens up around me and within me. There is room for inspiration, for peace, and for new solutions to reach me, even on the most difficult days.

ENDLESS POSSIBILITIES

Whenever I find myself at a crossroads—facing a difficult decision, clinging to limiting beliefs (those inner stories and assumptions that restrict what we believe is possible for ourselves), or feeling weighed down by the state of the world or my own life—I think of the river.

A river has a shape, a course, a presence we recognize as a single, continuous entity. Just as we think of ourselves as "me," we see the river as something defined and whole. Yet its true nature is movement: an ever-changing flow held within the structure of its banks. Like the cells in our bodies, which are constantly renewing, the river is never the same from one moment to the next. And within its current, the possibilities are endless.

I have seen countless forms of life held by the river: fish, insects, beavers, and birds both migratory and local. Once, to my amazement, I watched a squirrel swim all the way across. Another time, I spotted what, from a distance, looked like a shark fin gliding through the water, only to be amazed when a deer emerged and stepped onto the shore.

I've also witnessed a rich array of boats, from tiny rowboats to massive barges hauling equipment. Trees and tires have floated by. Once, a lifeless cow appeared to be tangled in fallen branches. Concerned, I took a picture with my telephoto zoom lens. But when I examined it later on my laptop, seams were visible. It was a cow costume! I am also fairly certain the river once carried off one of our kayaks.

One summer day, I longed to hold a water lily in my hands and place it on my meditation altar but couldn't bring myself to cut one from the river garden. On my next paddle, a single white water lily drifted toward me as if the river had delivered it as a gift. That only happened once. Another time, a bald eagle feather floated by—just once. It felt like part of that day's remarkable conversation between the river and me.

There have been incredible moments of inspiration on this waterway. One day, I encountered a hand-built shanty boat collecting stories from river communities, not just on the Hudson but across the country. Another day, internationally esteemed endurance swimmer and environmental ambassador, Lewis Pugh, swam by. He was only the second person known to swim the entire length of the Hudson. Both encounters reminded me of the river's power to inspire human greatness, whether through bold feats of endurance or the vision and artistry to create a floating storytelling vessel.

There was also the massive PCBs dredging project, which took place right in front of our house and invoked a sense of awe.

Then there are the small, steady rhythms of the river: the flotillas of fallen autumn leaves and drifting cottonwood seeds in spring, traveling downriver in search of fertile ground.

The river is full of surprises. It carries inspiration, metaphors, guidance, and endless possibilities. There is always something new to discover, something waiting to expand our understanding.

I try to remember this whenever limiting beliefs take hold of me. Like the river, life is always in motion. You never know what might come floating your way to awaken new ways of seeing and being.

Like the river, we are always changing, too.

MAYBE

Maybe it's not the sunrise sky.
Maybe it's the way the budding trees
are silhouetted by the angle of backlight
or the sound of a woodpecker across the river
adding a touch of percussion
to the songbird symphony.

Maybe it's not the great blue heron.
Maybe it's the cluster of forget-me-nots
growing from a rocky wall
as you paddle by.

Maybe it's not reaching a certain
destination or state of mind.
Maybe it's the sound of your paddle
dipping into calm, reflective water
or the feel of each footstep
meeting the ground.

Maybe it's not the white swan
but the way it inspired you
to pay closer attention,
and to have enough faith
to take the next step.

Maybe it wasn't getting the shot.
Maybe it was simply being there
experiencing what was,
instead of longing for
what wasn't.

Maybe waiting for the sun
to emerge from or duck behind a cloud
is an invitation to notice
some small, lovely thing
that otherwise would have
remained unseen.

Maybe it's not something tiny
but the whole wide landscape
including you sitting or standing,
part of it all, breathing.

Maybe it's not a sight but a sound
or an opportunity to adjust
the focus, the angle, the depth
of your field of awareness.

Maybe what you were seeking
was just one of many possibilities,
and your unmet expectations
are a gateway to something greater.

Maybe it's not about happy-ever-after.
Maybe it's feeling alive, engaged
with the magic of this fleeting,
ever-present now.

Maybe what you set off in search of
isn't what you will find.
Maybe its purpose
was to lead you here.

REFLECTING STILLNESS

I love it when the river is calm and reflective, like glass. Visually, it's like twice as much of a good thing. A radiant sunrise, doubled. But it also imparts something deeper: a calm, reflective inner quality that mirrors the outer scene. I usually wait for tranquil water before heading out in my kayak. The river is my reflective place, and I enjoy gliding through, and floating quietly amid, its clear reflections.

Zen master Thich Nhat Hanh offered many breathing verses, or *gathas*, drawn from the natural world.[17] One that comes to mind often is:

> *Breathing in, I see myself as still water.*
> *Breathing out, I reflect things as they truly are.*

And a variation:

> *Breathing in, I see myself as still water.*
> *Breathing out, I feel calm.*

Each of us has still water inside of us, and we can touch it with the breath by pausing and coming home to ourselves, allowing the mind to settle. When our mind is reactive or upset, it's like the surface of the river when it's choppy: It doesn't reflect things as they really are. But when it becomes calm and still, it mirrors the trees, the sky, and everything around it with near-perfect clarity.

A still, peaceful mind benefits not only ourselves but also those around us. As William Butler Yeats wrote:

We can make our minds so like still water that beings gather about us that they may see, it may be, their own images, and so live for a moment with a clearer, perhaps even with a fiercer life because of our quiet.[18]

Thoughts and emotions are like waves on the surface, distorting our view and stirring up confusion and suffering. But beneath those waves, the deeper waters remain calm. This is true of both the river and the mind. Thinking is only a small part of consciousness. Beneath the swirl of thought, there is a spacious stillness we can return to that offers clarity, insight, and ease.

When I feel uncertain or overwhelmed, I take it to the river. The outer calm awakens an inner calm. And when it is not possible to physically be on the water, I can call up a mental image or turn to one of the river photographs displayed around my home. That is the power of visual art: It reminds us of what we value, how we want to feel, the qualities we want to embody.

I am amazed every time something hidden in plain sight suddenly comes into view. It might be something I have passed by many times but now feel drawn to like a magnet. Two moments come to mind.

Normally, I wait for the water to become smooth as glass before photographing the river. It takes patience; every paddle stroke creates ripples. But one day, I became captivated by the reflections *during* the disturbance. The distorted shapes shimmered like abstract art. Pausing, I watched them gradually settle into coherence. Something new to appreciate.

That day, I spent a long time paddling and pausing, photographing and filming the water as it slowly returned to stillness. Breathing with the wavering reflections and feeling my own mind settle as the surface cleared became a visual meditation.

Another time, I photographed a spot where the water was very shallow. Beneath the surface were scattered leaves, while above it, branches and foliage cast crisp reflections. Looking at the image later, I couldn't immediately tell what was real and what was reflection. It was like a riddle, with illusion and reality layered into one composition.

We often assume we are seeing things clearly, just as they are. But moments like this remind me to stop and ask: *Am I sure?*

Sometimes, the clarity we seek doesn't come from doing, but from pausing. From questioning the assumptions we make and the adjectives we use. From allowing the mind to settle.

The river reminds me that the stillness is already here. We just have to stop stirring the water.

TEARS

Once I took my sorrow to the river,
paddled away from human noise
to a quiet place—and cried.
I watched my tears splash,
create ripples, and become
part of the collective:
no longer "mine"
or separate in any way.

Suddenly I didn't feel alone
anymore or misunderstood.
Floating in my kayak, held
and carried by a gentle current,
I recognized each drop of water
that forms the river
as a tear someone cried
perhaps once, perhaps
millions of times.

After my tears subsided
I paddled home on a river
of shared humanity,
in a world connected by oceans
and clouds and tears.
For a short time, I stopped
believing lonely tales
of you and me
and us and them.
And for a time, I was free.

SEATED BY THE RIVER

When I see a parade of autumn leaves, cottonwood seeds, or plates of ice drifting downriver, it brings to mind the stream of thought.

If you were to sit on the riverside looking straight ahead, whatever flows down the river simply comes and goes. It's like having a video camera mounted on a tripod, recording whatever passes through the stationary frame. And when something leaves the frame, it's gone. It continues on its way.

But if you turn your head to follow what is floating by—perhaps a boat—it stays in view longer. You give it more attention instead of just letting it pass. You might even begin tracking it when it is still upstream.

It's just like that when you get caught in the stream of thought during meditation. The moment you "get on the boat" or follow it down the river, you are no longer seated on the riverside. You have been carried away.

Getting carried away is natural. The question is: How far down the river will you get before you realize? Mindfulness helps you to realize sooner and to remember that you can return.

Human minds often time-travel to the future or to the past. Looking upstream is like imagining what might be coming. Looking downstream is like focusing on what already has passed. But true presence is simply facing forward. Letting each moment enter the frame, float through it, and move on.

When you notice your mind has wandered into memory, imagination, planning, or replaying, you don't need to judge it. It's what human minds do. Just return to your seat by the river, and gently turn your head back to center. Let what flows by, flow by. No need to anticipate or hold onto anything.

Release your thoughts to the current.

OPENING TO THE SOUNDSCAPE

Despite living in the countryside, our stretch of the Upper Hudson is not particularly quiet. A truck route runs alongside the river, and there is nearly constant transportation noise from cars, motorcycles, farm vehicles, and the loudest of all: tank trucks. The nearby steel deck bridge also hums with vibration each time a vehicle crosses.

After settling into my kayak, I instinctively paddle north, away from the bridge and the road that hugs the riverbank. Still, it's surprising how far that noise carries. And as I paddle away from one busy road, sounds from another in the distance become more noticeable.

During the 2020 shutdown, something remarkable happened: The road noise hushed. In the stillness, nature's sounds emerged more clearly: birds, wind, water lapping the shore. They had always been there, but now it was easier to hear them. Their song was both music to my ears and a doorway out of mental chatter and into deeper stillness. When I found myself absorbed in thinking, birdsong brought me back. Like a meditation bell or anchor, it returned me to presence many times a day.

When businesses reopened, the return of road noise hit me hard. I felt more sensitive to it than ever before, startled by how loud and harsh it seemed. I longed for the gentle, layered symphony of rustling leaves, flowing water, treetop warblers.

But mindfulness has taught me that what feels like an obstacle is often the path itself. So, I turned toward the sound. Rather than resist, I chose to practice with it.

The first step is awareness: simply noticing the sounds comprising the soundscape. I listen with curiosity, not trying to filter out the unpleasant or amplify the beautiful, but receiving all of it, like a recording device that doesn't judge what it captures. I practice being a receiver, effortlessly receiving. Then I bring awareness to how I am relating to the sounds. If a sound is pleasant, I let myself really soak it in, as if bathing in it. If it is a fleeting, seasonal joy, like spring peepers or migrating geese, I savor its impermanence.

Often, it's the unpleasant sounds that call me most clearly to practice. One summer, the incessant trills and chirps of a male cardinal dominated the soundscape and provided plenty of opportunity. A loud truck or a leaf blower might trigger tension, clenching, or the urge to flee. The resistance itself becomes the bell of mindfulness, a cue to open more fully to what is. I remind myself to include all sounds in the soundscape, whether intrusive or enjoyable.

The challenge becomes a kind of game: How long can I stay present with the sounds and the silence between them, without engaging the thinking mind? Can I allow it all—traffic, birdsong, wind, voices—to simply exist?

I can reflect on what the sounds signify from a broader perspective, beyond how they affect my river time. They are the sounds of people transporting heating fuel, groceries, supplies. They are the sounds of the interconnected web of life. I might even send a silent wish of lovingkindness to those inside the vehicles: *May you travel safely. May your actions benefit others.*

Insight emerges from observing my mind's patterns over time. When tracking a pleasant sound like birdsong, do I lose that thread of awareness when a less agreeable sound cuts in, and fixate on the undesired noise? Can I still hear the river's soft music, or have my thoughts drowned it out?

When recording video or audio on the river, I become almost hyper-aware of the soundscape and my reactivity toward it. This is another wonderful invitation to practice. I might hope for uninterrupted birdsong, only to hear a plane overhead. Or the wind might pick up, turning the microphone into a fluttering drum of distortion that drowns out everything else. Frustration itself becomes a mindfulness bell, reminding me that I have another choice: to practice open, receptive awareness. Even if the recording is "ruined," my capacity for equanimity has grown.

Mindfulness doesn't ask us to eliminate disturbance. It invites us to remain peaceful within it. That is true freedom. Can I let go of resistance and simply enjoy being on the river? And when that is hard, can I remember that contrast can be a gift that helps us grow—and practice changing how I relate to jarring sounds?

I've even come to notice that certain traffic sounds resemble ocean waves. The shift in perception that reframes the noise makes it easier to stay present. It's not just the sound itself that pulls us out of presence, but how we react to it. We tense, compare, wish things were different. But the moment we notice our reactivity, we are already back in awareness. We can say, "Ah, I see you, resistance," and soften.

When we recognize our role in creating unnecessary suffering, something beautiful happens: We reclaim our power. We begin to feel more connected to the world, even amid what once felt like disturbance.

Being on the river becomes more joyful when I let the full soundscape belong. I don't need to control the music of the moment like a conductor. I am just one instrument in the symphony. Sometimes my part is silence. Sometimes it's the gentle sounds of paddling through water.

There will always be sound. There will always be contrast. But I can choose how to listen and how to live. The practice of mindful listening can help us be more inclusive and less reactive, while strengthening our relationship with the world around us.

Zen master Thich Nhat Hanh offered a simple mindfulness verse that is also the title of one of his books: *Present Moment,*

Wonderful Moment.[19] The present moment truly can be wonderful. It all depends on the quality of our attention. With awareness, we can choose not only what we give our attention to, but our attitude toward it.

We can practice allowing whatever arises to be part of the river experience, free ourselves from the suffering of resistance, and soak in the joy of our peaceful place.

BACK TO THE SENSES

This is a happy moment.
Carried by a strong breeze,
lilac blossoms perfume the air.
River reflects deep blue sky
and sparkles with sunlight.
The current is strong.
A Baltimore oriole leads
the birdsong symphony.
This breakfast in my kayak
is nourishing and delicious.

Even so, the restless mind
wanders, looking for trouble—
gets too close to the river
and is carried away
by habit energy.
Just like that, life grows
complicated again:
no longer smelling,
tasting, hearing, seeing,
touching what is
here to be known.

This morning, the river flows
in both directions—
to past and future.
Each breath is a lifeline back
to the senses, to this body:
an invitation to begin again.

LET IT GO, LET IT FLOW

It was the first full day of spring. I sat at my desk overlooking the river, writing about an idea that was alive in me: the importance of tending to the roots of war within ourselves, so we don't contribute to disharmony in the world. Even when we feel powerless in the face of the world's suffering, there is always something we can do to generate peace.

Can we be honest with ourselves about the roots of conflict inside us? Wherever there is disharmony, whether it is toward another person or within ourselves, can we acknowledge it and seek to heal it? In doing so, we might bring a little more harmony into the world. It's about letting go of the ego's need to be right or to fixate on the negative qualities in others. Can we simply let go?

This does not mean we need to be closer to others or even in contact with them at all. It can all be done internally. Let go of the stories you tell about people. Let go of the "otherness" that you use to define yourself or position yourself as better than. There is so much we can let go of, to become part of a ripple of peace in the world.

I paused from writing and looked out at the river. The current was strong, and as I watched, a large plate of ice floated by. That image spoke to me deeply. It seemed to reflect exactly what I was writing about: letting go. Letting go of the things, big and small, that don't serve inner or outer peace.

So I stopped what I was doing to watch the ice plate drift down the river. The words that came to me were clear: *Let it go. Let it flow.* Release to the river whatever doesn't serve peace. The river will take care of it.

I went outside to track the ice plate. As it rounded a bend under the bridge, I got in my car and drove to a spot near the dam, to watch the river do its work. I waited there, eager to see the ice plate pass over the dam and get broken down until it wasn't this big chunk of ego anymore. It was just part of the river.

A voice inside me cheered. It was something gratifying to witness.

HOLD THE ROPE

From time to time, it's fun to go through the canal locks in my kayak. It is quite an experience. The immense doors creak open like an ancient castle drawbridge lowering with the weight of history—slow, groaning, deliberate. You paddle in, perhaps alone or with larger boats, and make your way to one of the side walls.

A lock is like a cross between a giant bathtub and an elevator. The chamber fills with or empties water, to lift or lower vessels to the next stretch of river. As the water level rises or falls, the surface churns and swirls with great force, like water circling a drain.

Fortunately, there are thick drop ropes along the side walls to hold onto for stability. Without them, especially in a small kayak, you would get jostled and spun about by the turbulence. Those ropes are essential.

I like to think of the mind as a lock chamber, and thoughts as the swirling water. A meditative anchor (the breath, for example) is the rope. It offers steadiness. When things inside feel chaotic or stirred up, returning to the breath is like reaching out and finding that rope again. When we are holding the rope, we are not swept away by the whirlpool of thought.

Water often symbolizes emotion. It can rise and fall, swell and churn. And just as the lock must fill or drain before we can move forward, our emotions sometimes need to move through us before we can continue on. Thoughts often stir those waters, keeping them high or low. But holding the rope helps us return to equilibrium, allowing us to respond rather than react as we navigate the river of life.

Once, Jack and I were kayaking when the weather changed suddenly. The sky darkened, and thunder began to rumble. We realized we needed to head home quickly or find shelter, but it turned out we were in the lock when the storm arrived. Lightning flashed overhead as the chamber filled with water. There was nowhere to go, nothing to do but wait it out. We each held our rope and breathed through the storm.

It was scary. And it taught us to be more mindful, not just of the weather forecast, but of subtler shifts in the sky and wind. Not all storms come suddenly; some arrive quietly, with clues noticed only by a present, observant mind.

That storm became a lesson in both outer and inner weather. We can't always control what arises, but we can steady ourselves. We can notice the signs. We can hold the rope.

Zoom Out

September sunrises are my favorite. This is one of many realizations I've had after seventeen years of photographing Hudson River sunrises, including an entire year of photographing virtually *every* dawn.

What is it about September sunrises that makes them so remarkable, both visually and metaphorically? Beginning with the most obvious answer . . .

Fog.

Some mornings, the fog is so thick that the landscape disappears entirely; only gradations of shadow and light remain. But no matter how dense the fog, eventually it lifts. This is inevitable.

On foggy mornings, I bring more than one camera or photography technique to the riverside, hoping to capture different aspects of the unfolding scene. My professional camera, equipped with a wide-angle lens, frames the fog in a way that makes it seem endless. But I can go wider, using my phone's panorama function or stitching together multiple vertical images from my camera.

I enjoy comparing these images, noticing their differences. There is something satisfying about it, a deeper resonance that suggests the natural world is mirroring something about life itself.

Inevitably, we all experience times of uncertainty, when clarity eludes us, like being lost in a fog of confusion. We search for answers, but they remain obscured, just beyond reach. Such moments can feel frustrating, as if the fog will never lift. But rest assured: *This, too, will pass.*

Often, the problem is that we are too close to the issue, too identified with our confusion. In such moments, we can take a wider view.

When we expand our perspective, we remember that beyond the fog, there is always blue sky; the fog isn't endless. The spacious sky of clarity and illumination of sunlight still exist behind the fog that comes and goes.

We can learn to identify with clear-sky consciousness rather than the fog that moves through it, clouding our vision. The key is to recognize when we are immersed in a thought-fog and remember the transient nature of thoughts and feelings.

The sky is vast, steady, and ever-present, while the fog is fleeting. That is what I see in super-wide images of foggy river sunrises. They remind me that consciousness is larger than the fog and clouds that pass through every human life.

When faced with an unresolved issue, try expanding your field of awareness. Seek out a vast landscape: ocean, mountains, big sky. If you don't have access to such a view, imagine one in rich detail. Experience yourself as a tiny speck within an expansive scene.

This shift in perspective mirrors the difference between two types of photographs: one taken from my own vantage point as I glide through the river in my kayak, and another taken from a distance, where the kayak is merely a dot in a sweeping landscape. The latter reminds me that I am part of something much greater.

Once you have widened your perspective, breathe deeply, and bring to mind the issue that weighs on you. As awareness expands beyond the boundaries of your physical body and even beyond the walls of your home, space opens up for insight and wisdom to emerge and *be received*. You might even visualize a foggy landscape clearing as the fog lifts. Surround yourself with space, keep breathing, and be patient with the process.

Although thinking is an addiction for many, we are so much more than a relentless stream of thought. Expanding awareness to a wider field allows us to access consciousness beyond thought: intuition, inspiration, synchronicity.

An answer or insight might arise as if out of thin air, when we release ourselves from the thought-stream. A tree or an animal we have seen countless times but never really noticed may suddenly stand out as if carrying a message. A possibility we never considered might come into view. Guidance comes in so many ways! We can come to know thinking as a small part of consciousness and remember to return to spacious awareness when we are immersed in thought.

This is the difference between being *mindful* and having a *mind full*. Since the two phrases sound identical, I often prefer the word *presence*.

Foggy sunrises also illuminate the evanescent nature of all worldly things, including us. Everything changes. If you sit by the river long enough and really pay attention, you will witness the slow dance of fog rising, shifting shape, and becoming clouds or dissolving into the sky. It is breathtaking.

So far, I have focused on widening perspective through space—zooming out to see more. But we also can expand our view through time.

Imagine yourself years into the future, or even at the end of your life, as the future self you aspire to be. From that vantage point, look back on your current situation. What does this desired future version of you want present-day you to know? When seen through the lens of an entire lifetime, what truly matters?

So, it's not just a beautiful landscape that propels me out of bed and to the river's edge on cool, foggy, September mornings. It's the revelations packaged within it, hidden in plain sight, waiting to be unwrapped. Reminders to

❖ zoom out, both in space and time, to access greater clarity and insight

❖ identify with the clear sky, ever-present beyond the ephemeral fog and clouds passing through it

❖ be patient when the way forward is unclear, trusting that insight and guidance will emerge as the fog lifts.

WHERE DOES THE RIVER BEGIN AND END?

Z en master Thich Nhat Hanh coined the term *interbeing* to describe the deep insight that we are not separate from the environment. No being exists in isolation; none of us is an island. The existence of everything and everyone depends on myriad others. We are interdependent with each other and with the earth.

Spending time on the river being truly present has offered me so many moments of seeing this truth firsthand. One morning in early autumn, I paddled through a curtain of fog, the air cool on my face, the water still as glass. A pair of geese lifted off the shoreline and disappeared into the mist, their calls echoing over the water. And I was part of it all. For a moment, I felt the boundaries between the river and me dissolve.

I love being on the water and living beside it but often wonder: What exactly do I mean when I say "river"? Floating in my kayak, held by the river and the landscape around it, I begin to question where the river actually begins and ends.

Looking at a map, you might say the Hudson begins at Lake Tear of the Clouds, on the southwest slope of Mount Marcy in the Adirondack Mountains, and ends where it enters the Atlantic Ocean through New York Harbor. But there is so much more to the river than a starting point and an endpoint, the banks on either side, and the bed below.

The shore sometimes becomes part of the river, just as the beach you walk at low tide disappears beneath the ocean at high tide.

The surface of the water is part of the river. When it is calm, it reflects the clouds, the trees, the birds above, even the stars at night. Its appearance shifts with the weather: gray under cloudy skies, deep blue on a clear day, brown and murky after a heavy rain.

Below the surface, fish dart through the water. Turtles brumate in the mud at the bottom of the river during winter, or shelter beneath submerged logs. Aren't they part of the river, too?

Sounds belong to the river: the splash of a wave hitting shore, the squawking of a heron, the chorus of frogs at dusk. Waves can't lap a shore that isn't there. Sound requires space and movement. It requires relationship.

Water makes up more than half of our body. All the water on the planet is part of a great recycling process: the water cycle. When I am kayaking, droplets fall from my paddle and return to the river to become part of the whole again—no longer a single drop. I find this endlessly moving. The water cycle seems to mirror something essential about our own nature.

Fog rises from the river, becomes clouds, drifts across the sky, and falls again as rain, perhaps somewhere far away. Tears can be seen as recycled river water. Reciprocally, the river contains our tears, too.

Great blue herons, ospreys, and eagles live along these waters. They are part of the river's story. And so am I. Paddling down the river gives the impression of being large in relation to my surroundings, much like a figure standing in between the projector and the movie screen, casting an imposing shadow on the scene. But I long to see myself from a distance, from the view of a bird or a friend standing on shore. I want to see my true scale, not separate from my surroundings, but a small part of the whole landscape that does not revolve around me. Once, when I was photographing a sunset on the seashore, someone photographed me in this way, and it was a real gift.

I have watched herons and egrets gulp down fish swimming in PCB-contaminated water, only to fly south in the fall, carrying traces of that pollution with them. It reminds me that nothing truly stays in one place. Our actions ripple outward. A river cannot be separated from the rest of the world. It flows into the ocean, which connects with every other ocean. All of it is part of one great body: the World Ocean.

We are like that, too: boundless and interconnected. Who are we, and where do we begin and end? The river reminds me that the answer isn't always clear. There are innumerable non-river elements that shape what we experience as the river. And there are innumerable non-us elements that form what we call "me"—our mind, our body, our experience. We are shaped by countless forces we cannot control and did not choose. And in turn, our actions send ripples into the world, like a boat passing through water.

I am part of the river. You are, too.

After I am gone, if you visit this quiet stretch where I have spent so many hours, so many years, you might find me here still—in the shimmer of light on the water, in the dance of the fog, in the flight of a heron, in the blooming of a water lily. In everything I have loved. Maybe you will love it, too.

We are part of everything we love, and everything we love is part of us. When we share a love of something in nature, we form new connections, both with the world and with each other.

River Bliss*

What did you notice that stirred brightness in you?
    The river flowing free again, its winter blanket melted;
    trail of sparkling sunlight stretched before my kayak,
    inviting me to follow it back home;
    waves of light projected onto a riverside tree,
    streaming from the branches into the heart of the trunk;
    stars and fireflies twinkling above and reflected below;
    golden oak leaves and crimson maples aglow
    like stained glass framed by deep blue sky.

What did you see that made you smile, soften, or fill with delight?
    White water lilies fully bloomed in the river garden;
    sunrise sky painting layers of clouds
    bright pink, tangerine, and lavender;
    sunlit sparkles on the water—like daytime fireflies;
    shoreline of spring trees bursting
    with the tender hues of baby leaves;
    ice formations sculpted and sketched along the shore;
    a dragonfly landing on my kayak, resting with me awhile;
    wisps of morning fog twirling like ballerinas
    on the river stage before lifting into the sky;
    a single feather floating past, glistening with dew.

This poem was inspired by a widely shared piece often titled "Gratitude," commonly attributed to Mary Oliver though not found in her published works. The structure and spirit of that poem guided these reflections.

What did you hear that touched your heart or made you feel alive?
Crackle of delicate ice pancakes tapping together
as they drift downstream;
gentle waves lapping at the shore;
leafy trees broadcasting cheerful birdsong;
leaves in the treetops shaking like soft tambourines
in a summer breeze.

What did you admire?
Great blue heron's steady concentration;
beaver setting clear boundaries with a firm slap of its tail.

What did you smell that brought you more fully into the moment?
Sweet perfume of milkweed blossoms;
remembered fragrance of lilies-of-the-valley
from childhood gardens.

What astonished or surprised you?
The river floating a water lily to me
as if in appreciation of my music;
mass of delicate ice plates sliding over patterned
shoreline ice, layering intricate designs;
bald eagle's feather carried beside me on the current;
stunning sunset after a storm, when the sky
had seemed hopelessly overcast;
gray squirrel swimming across the wide river;
shadows of current flowing visibly across sunlit leaves;
the veins on lily pads forming the shape of a water lily;
a fleet of hot air balloons drifting closer than ever before;
the sheer size of an eagle's nest overlooking the river.

What felt most wonderful?
  The cool breath of morning air
  before summer's heat awakens;
  warmth of sunlight on a crisp day;
  raindrops shaking from trees
  like a refreshing mist when the breeze stirs.

What tenderness did you experience?
  Adult geese guiding their goslings protectively
  from front and behind, floating in a family line;
  ethereal beauty of frosted trees on the riverside
  when my mother was ill;
  slender red columbines and forget-me-nots
  blooming from hard rock walls along the river.

What would you love to experience again?
  Shimmering aurora borealis reflected
  on water's calm, glassy surface;
  paddling under the light of the full moon;
  discovering a statuesque heron in the fog;
  a cloud shaped distinctly like an angel—
  just like the one from a dream the night before;
  the first day on the river in springtime,
  with a whole season ahead.

EPILOGUE:
THE RIVER WITHIN

It is the summer of 2025, and I haven't been on the river as much as usual this year. Many days have been too rainy, too hot, or too windy. There's also been a lot of smoke from Canadian wildfires compromising air quality. As much as possible, I position myself by a window with a view of the river, pausing from my activities to watch the water flow. The view alone is something to be grateful for, even when conditions are not favorable for kayaking.

Time on the water is something I miss, especially in a year as challenging as this one. But some years are like that. One of the lessons I have learned from the river is that there is a time to paddle and a time to go with the flow. Since the weather cannot be changed at will, this has been a go-with-the-flow year.

During my yearlong sunrise photography project, my appreciation for the river only deepened. Dreams about moving away from the river for one reason or another sometimes haunted my sleep. One ended with me narrating, "The saddest words are *I lived on the river.*" It felt unbearable to imagine life without river access and the current flowing outside my door. Waking up to realize it was just a dream always came as a relief.

In some dreams, appreciation was the dominant feeling tone: How could I possibly take a single moment of living on the river for granted? I was acutely aware of both the privilege it is to live here and witness the daily rhythms of the river, and the realization that all things will pass.

Before falling in love with the river, waterfalls were my refuge. For several years earlier in life, I lived in Ithaca, New York, where the slogan is: *Ithaca is Gorges*. Within a ten-mile radius of Ithaca, more than 150 waterfalls cascade through the gorges.

Hiking through the gorges and writing poetry at the base of favorite waterfalls was a cherished practice. Back then, I believed poetry flowed best near falling water. After moving away, I discovered that wasn't true. I missed those waterfalls deeply but carried their memory within me. Whenever I wanted to visualize a peaceful, safe place in nature, Cascadilla Gorge or Ithaca Falls returned vividly. And when I visit Ithaca now, not a single footstep through the gorges is taken for granted.

Now I am out on the river as the sun is setting. A path of sunlight stretches across the water like a trail of diamonds. Tears stream down my cheeks; my heart is full. I love this river and the state of being it helps me to access.

In both waking life and dreams, the river becomes a metaphor for life itself. To live with steadfast appreciation would be a game-changer: recognizing what we have, knowing it is enough, and understanding it is all impermanent. And being at peace with the latter because it is simply the nature of life.

The insight of impermanence can generate gratitude and clarity. None of us is guaranteed tomorrow, so why not appreciate the gift of this life now? We cannot stop the river of life from flowing as it does. What matters is how we relate to it. Releasing resistance to the ever-changing circumstances of life allows us to be more present to its preciousness and more attuned to the flow of our deeper wisdom. Clear presence empowers us to live more fully into our human potential while we still can.

Appreciation is how I aspire to live each day. Appreciate it all, because it all will pass. Even the experiences that were painful at the time help us grow, if we're willing to learn from them. They played a role in our awakening.

The unpleasant dreams revealed just how attached I had become to living on the river. Clinging is disempowering and breeds suffering. The antidote is cultivating *non-attachment*, which is neither detachment nor disinterest but the capacity to allow all things to come and go. It is essential because impermanence is the nature of all worldly things.

There are certain places where we find the nourishment we long for most. Yet what we eventually discover, often through loss or change, is that the nourishment we seek in these places isn't located there. What we're truly longing for is already within us. People and places may help us find it, but they are not the source. They are different pathways home.

The creative receptivity I experienced around waterfalls also flows in peaceful moments on the river, by the ocean, or in the woods. It's the same current of being, accessible in different landscapes.

After my parents died, I was amazed to feel closer to them than ever before. Their presence had become part of me: clear voices in my heart. In the vast ocean heart within us, love is never lost. Everything and everyone we have ever loved becomes part of us. And with the insight of interbeing, we realize they always were.

In my twenties, hospice volunteer training encouraged me to reflect on aging and the possibility of someday having limited mobility. At the time, I was devoted to rigorous daily exercise and could not imagine life without it.

Becoming a mother shifted that priority. Caring for my daughter became more important than fitness routines. I still exercised, but in more accessible ways, such as hiking with her in a baby carrier backpack. That was my first lesson in how our brains, hormones, and values change through different seasons of life. We adapt. What matters most in one chapter of life won't necessarily carry through to the next. I find this reassuring.

The voice in our heads is almost always saying something, but the thoughts aren't necessarily accurate. It wasn't true that I needed to be near a waterfall to write a satisfying poem. Moving away from Ithaca was painful, but had it not happened, I wouldn't have discovered the deep connection I now have with the river.

If the time ever comes to leave the river, I trust my capacity to adapt. Even as I write those words, resistance rises; I don't want to leave. The discomfort of resistance is another mindfulness bell, signaling something is out of alignment and needs attention.

Through all these years of living, I have come to trust something deeper than my thoughts or fears: the inner space and stillness beneath them. So, I practice catching and releasing diminishing thoughts and resting in the boundless presence that can hold all the twists and turns of life. It is a practice, and I certainly have not mastered it. But I trust the part of me where rivers and waterfalls flow eternally, as close as my own heart. It is the place where everyone and everything I have ever loved still lives. When we access that place within, we can be at home wherever we are, because we are at home in ourselves.

Notes

Preface

1. Henry David Thoreau, *I to Myself: An Annotated Selection from the Journal of Henry D. Thoreau*, ed. Jeffrey S. Cramer (Yale University Press, 2007), 182.

Part 1

2. Thich Nhat Hanh, *No Mud, No Lotus: The Art of Transforming Suffering* (Parallax Press, 2014).

3. Kathleen Cain, *The Cottonwood Tree: An American Champion* (Bower House, 2007).

4. Hazrat Inayat Khan, "Chalas," *Gayan, Vadan, Nirtan*. Wahiduddin's Web, accessed March 16, 2025, https://wahiduddin.net/mv2/say/gayan_chalas.htm.

5. Doris Stickney, *Water Bugs and Dragonflies: Explaining Death to Young Children* (Pilgrim Press, 1982).

Part 2

6. "EPA's Third Five-Year Review of the Upper Hudson River Cleanup Hudson River PCBs Superfund Site," Environmental Protection Agency (January 2025), accessed March 28, 2025, https://www.epa.gov/system/files/documents/2025-01/hudson_final3rdfyr_factsheet_english_2.pdf.

7. "Fact Sheet 11," Hudson River Sloop Clearwater, accessed March 29, 2025, https://www.clearwater.org/news/dredge.html.

8. "Environmental Groups Condemn EPA's Final Review of the Hudson Superfund Site," Riverkeeper (January 17, 2025), accessed March 29, 2025, https://www.riverkeeper.org/news-and-events/news-and-updates/environmental-groups-condemn-epa-s-final-review-of-the-hudson-superfund-site.

9. Susan Fenimore Cooper, "The Hudson River and its Early Names," *The Magazine of American History*, 4, no. 6 (1880): 401-418, https://jfcoopersociety.org/content/03-life/susan/hudson.htm?tocpath=Susan%20Fenimore%20Cooper%7C_____9

10. Mrs. J. B. (Grace) VanDerwerker, *Early Days in Eastern Saratoga County* (Heart of the Lakes Publishing, 1994).

11. A Secret History of American River People, accessed May 8, 2025, https://peoplesriverhistory.org/.

12. Alfred Lansing. *Endurance: Shackleton's Incredible Voyage* (Basic Books, 2015).

13. Henry Wadsworth Longfellow, *Prose Works of Henry Wadsworth Longfellow*, Volume 1 (Boston, 1857), 452.

Part 3

14. "The Five Mindfulness Trainings," Plum Village, accessed May 18, 2025, https://plumvillage.org/mindfulness/the-5-mindfulness-trainings.

15. Hafiz, *The Subject Tonight Is Love*, trans. Daniel Ladinsky (Pumpkin House, 1996).

16. Gibran, Kahlil, *The Prophet* (New York, 1923).

Part 4

17. Thich Nhat Hanh, "New Mindfulness Verse," *The Mindfulness Bell*, no. 4, (1991), accessed May 12, 2025, https://www.parallax.org/mindfulnessbell/article/new-mindfulness-verse/.

18. William Butler Yeats, *The Celtic Twilight: Faerie and Folklore* (London, 1902).

19. Thich Nhat Hanh, *Present Moment, Wonderful Moment* (Parallax Press, 1990).

ACKNOWLEDGMENTS

N o book is brought into being in isolation. Like the river that flows through these pages, this work has been nourished by many tributaries of inspiration and kindness. I offer my deepest gratitude to those who have helped guide its course.

To my friends and sangha sisters Shannon Snyder and Melissa Devine: Thank you for reading early drafts and offering thoughtful feedback. Your encouragement meant so much. And to Starr Regan DiCuircio, who traveled the author's path before me and generously shared her wisdom and feedback: Thank you for lighting the way.

A deep bow to the teachers who have shaped my path, beginning with David Pitkin, who set me on the spiritual path in junior high school and was, for decades, like a second father to me. His influence remains indelible more than a decade after he shed his physical form. And to my dear religious studies professor from Ithaca College and longtime spiritual director, Alice McDowell, whose steadfast presence is one of life's great blessings. I also bow in gratitude to Thich Nhat Hanh, Jack Kornfield, and Tara Brach, whose teachings continue to guide and inspire my life and practice.

To the participants in my meditation classes: Thank you for walking this path of presence with me and encouraging me to write this book. You remind me daily why this work matters.

To my family: Thank you for standing behind me through this entire process. Deep appreciation to my husband, Jack, who has always encouraged me to follow my heart (and who took the pictures of me found in this book); to my adult children, Jasmine and Cianan, for your steady encouragement; and to my granddaughter, Ava, whose inquiries about how the book was coming along, and delight at the idea of her grandma being an author, offered an extra dose of motivation.

Thank you to my awesome coach, Jaya, for your constant encouragement.

I'd also like to thank the anonymous soul who left a "random act of kindness" package on my doorstep just after Thanksgiving. Inside was James Crews' beautiful book, *Unlocking the Heart: Writing for Mindfulness, Courage, and Self-Compassion.* It was the perfect inspiration at the perfect time. Writing this book had long been a dream and a goal for the new year, and your gift gave me the push I needed to begin in earnest. You know who you are, even if I don't. This is a beautiful reminder of how small acts of kindness can have a profound impact.

And thank YOU, dear reader, for picking up this book and spending some time on the river with me.

ABOUT THE AUTHOR

SUSAN MEYER is a meditation teacher, photographer, and contemplative creative living in upstate New York.

She has been meditating for nearly forty years and has trained with Tara Brach and Jack Kornfield, completing both their Mindfulness Meditation Teacher Certification Program and Mindfulness Mentor Training. She is also an aspirant for ordination in the Tiep Hien Order (Order of Interbeing), founded by Zen master Thich Nhat Hanh.

Susan teaches meditation and nature photography, offers mindfulness mentoring and coaching, and is a teacher on the Insight Timer app. She created a self-paced, online course, *Resource Your Life with the Magic of Mindfulness*, and two inspirational card decks pairing contemplative insights with her nature images. Her nature photography has received multiple awards from the Erie Canalway National Heritage Corridor, and several of her images are featured on kiosks along the Empire State Trail in Schuylerville, New York.

She holds an M.A. in Education from Goddard College, a B.A. in Psychology from Ithaca College, and a Certificate in Spiritual Studies from the former Institute of Transpersonal Psychology (now Sofia University).

You can explore her work and sign up for her free newsletter at: **SusanTaraMeyer.com**.

Also from Susan Meyer

- ❖ *Mindful Nature Card Deck*
- ❖ *Loving Wisdom Card Deck*
- ❖ *Resource Your Life with the Magic of Mindfulness* (self-paced online course)

SUSANTARAMEYER.COM